Especially for

....

From

....

Date

....

The *12 Days* of *Christmas* COOKBOOK

2016 Edition

BARBOUR BOOKS
An Imprint of Barbour Publishing, Inc.

Published by Barbour Books, an imprint of Barbour Publishing, Inc., P.O. Box 719, Uhrichsville, Ohio, 44683, www.barbourbooks.com.

Our mission is to publish and distribute inspirational products offering exceptional value and biblical encouragement to the masses.

 Member of the
Evangelical Christian
Publishers Association

Printed in China.

Contents

Introduction

On the first day of Christmas my true love sent to me. . .

Take a deep breath and you can smell it in the air—
those intoxicating, delicious, and unique fragrances of
Christmas. The scent of fresh pine needles and candles,
along with favorite dishes wafting from the kitchen,
carry us back to childhood and all its delights. Those
special family recipes are such a great part of the spirit of
Christmas. This year we have included many recipes that
have been handed down for generations. We hope
they will bless you and your family as well.

*Father God, help us always remember that the joy in
Christmas is the joy of knowing that we have been
reconciled with You through the birth and death of
Your Son, Jesus—the greatest gift ever given. Amen.*

On the first day of Christmas my true love sent to me. . .

An Appetizer on a Platter

Christmas is a time for
"giving out," real giving, not swapping.

Unknown

Lord Jesus, thank You for Your magnificent gift, the greatest that could ever be given, free to all who will receive it. Thank You for giving Your life for ours, and in so doing, reconciling us to our Father, the Great Creator. If gifts are a sign of love, there is no greater love than Yours. Amen.

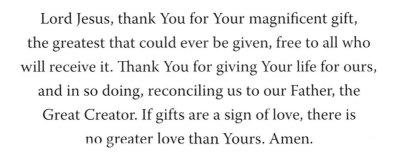

Jesus answered her, "If you knew the gift of God and who it is that asks you for a drink, you would have asked him and he would have given you living water."

JOHN 4:10 NIV

Cindy's Cheeseball

---

2 (8 ounce) packages cream cheese

½ bell pepper, diced

2 tablespoons onion, diced

1 tablespoon seasoned salt

2 (8 ounce) cans crushed pineapple, well drained

1 cup plus 2 tablespoons nuts (walnuts or pecans), chopped

Blend together all ingredients except 2 tablespoons nuts. Use hands to form mixture into ball. Place remaining nuts on wax paper. Roll cheeseball in nuts until covered. Refrigerate.

YIELD: 1 LARGE CHEESEBALL

Holiday Cheese Straws

---

1 (11 ounce) package piecrust mix

1½ cups extra-sharp cheddar cheese, shredded

1 teaspoon celery salt

¼ cup water

Combine piecrust mix, cheese, and celery salt. Mix well. Blend with water. Form into ball. Roll into 21 x 9-inch rectangle. Trim away 1 inch on all sides. Reserve trimmings. Divide rectangle in half to make two (20 x 4-inch) strips. Cut each into 4 x ½-inch strips. Reroll trimmings into a rectangle. Cut into strips. Twist each strip in a corkscrew fashion and place on cookie sheet covered with parchment paper. Bake for 8 to 10 minutes.

YIELD: 100 STRAWS

Snowman Dip

¼ cup heavy cream

2 cups cottage cheese, creamed

¼ cup carrot, grated

¼ cup green onion, thinly sliced

¼ cup green pepper, finely chopped

6 radishes, thinly sliced

¼ teaspoon black pepper

¼ teaspoon dill weed

Stir cream into cottage cheese. Add remaining ingredients. Mix well. Refrigerate. Serve with raw vegetables.

YIELD: 3 CUPS

Nutty Honey Brie

* · · · ❄ · · · ❄ · · · ❄ · · · *

1 (8 ounce) round of Brie cheese

¼ cup butter

¼ cup brown sugar, packed

¼ cup pecans, chopped

1 tablespoon honey

Preheat oven to 350 degrees. Place Brie in shallow pie plate and bake for 10 minutes. In saucepan, combine butter, brown sugar, pecans, and honey. Bring to a boil over medium heat, stirring constantly. Pour sauce over Brie. Cut into wedges.

Yield: 4 to 8 servings

Holiday Vegetable Tray

3 carrots

1 potato or turnip

10 radishes

1 bunch celery

1 bunch broccoli

1 head cauliflower

1 pint cherry tomatoes

2 bunches fresh parsley

⅔ cup sour cream

⅔ cup mayonnaise

¼ teaspoon dry mustard

1 tablespoon dry dill weed

1 tablespoon parsley, finely chopped

1 tablespoon onion, minced

Vegetables listed make a fine tray. Any vegetable can be added or subtracted based on preference. Cut into bite-sized pieces. Place on a round platter. Combine sour cream and remaining ingredients in small bowl. Chill. Serve together.

YIELD: 24 SMALL SERVINGS

Happy New Year Dip

½ pound cheddar cheese, cubed

1 cup butter, melted

4 cups black-eyed peas, drained

1 tablespoon jalapeño pepper, chopped

1 (4 ounce) can green chilies, chopped

1 clove garlic, minced

In saucepan over medium-low heat, melt cheese and butter, stirring frequently. Stir in peas, pepper, chilies, and garlic. Serve warm with crackers.

YIELD: 4 CUPS

Sweet Potato Balls

3 medium sweet potatoes, peeled and cut into quarters

½ teaspoon salt

½ teaspoon nutmeg

1 egg, beaten

1¼ cups pecans, finely chopped

¼ cup butter, melted

½ cup brown sugar, packed

3 tablespoons light corn syrup

Preheat oven to 375 degrees. Boil sweet potatoes until tender. Drain and mash. Add seasonings and mix well. Shape into ten 2-inch balls. Dip in egg. Roll in pecans. Place in baking dish. Combine butter, brown sugar, and corn syrup. Pour over balls. Bake for 20 minutes.

YIELD: 10 SERVINGS

Danny's Cheese Log

2 (8 ounce) packages cream cheese

2 cups cheddar cheese, shredded

1 (1 ounce) package ranch dressing mix

2½ cups pecans, chopped

Mix together cream cheese, cheddar cheese, and ranch dressing mix. Form into two logs, and roll in pecans. Refrigerate until firm.

YIELD: 2 LOGS

Cheesy Bacon Bites

½ pound sharp cheddar cheese

8 strips bacon, cut in half

¼ teaspoon cayenne pepper

8 cherry tomatoes, cut in half

Cut cheese into 16 cubes. Sprinkle with cayenne. Wrap bacon around each cheese cube. Secure with wooden toothpick. Place on baking sheet and broil for 5 minutes, turning once. Bacon should be cooked and cheese melting. When cool, add half a cherry tomato to each.

YIELD: 16 BITES

Spicy Nut Mix

¾ cup sugar

1 teaspoon cinnamon

¼ teaspoon allspice

¼ teaspoon nutmeg

½ teaspoon cloves

1 teaspoon salt

1 egg white

2½ tablespoons water

1 cup pecan halves

1 cup walnut halves

1 cup almonds, blanched

Preheat oven to 275 degrees. In small mixing bowl, combine sugar, spices, and salt. Beat egg white lightly and stir into sugar-spice mixture. Stir in water. Blend well. Add nuts about ½ cup at a time. Stir with fork to coat nuts well. Transfer nuts to greased baking sheet, separating each nut. Bake for 45 minutes. Remove from baking sheet with spatula. Store in airtight container.

YIELD: 3 CUPS

Chicken Sesame Bites

2 medium skinless chicken breasts, deboned

3 tablespoons lemon juice

2 tablespoons soy sauce

1 tablespoon sugar

1 tablespoon sherry

¼ cup butter

Toasted sesame seeds

Cut chicken breasts into 1-inch pieces and place in shallow dish. Combine lemon juice, soy sauce, sugar, and sherry. Pour over chicken. Allow to marinate for 30 minutes. Sauté chicken in butter for 5 minutes. Dip in sesame seeds. Serve with wooden picks.

YIELD: 4 DOZEN

Danish Meatballs

1 pound lean ground beef

2 eggs

1 tablespoon flour

1 large onion, chopped

½ cup milk

¼ teaspoon garlic, chopped

½ teaspoon Worcestershire sauce

¼ teaspoon pepper

½ teaspoon salt

1 tablespoon potato, grated

Combine all ingredients. Mix well. Fashion into balls. Fry in coconut oil.

Yield: 6 servings

Sausage Balls in Cranberry Sauce

1 pound seasoned pork sausage

2 eggs, beaten

1 cup fine bread crumbs

1 teaspoon salt

½ teaspoon poultry seasoning

1 (16 ounce) can jellied cranberry sauce

1 tablespoon prepared mustard

Preheat oven to 350 degrees. Combine sausage, eggs, bread crumbs, salt, and poultry seasoning. Shape into 1-inch balls. Bake for 30 minutes. Combine cranberry sauce and mustard in medium saucepan. Heat until melted. Add sausage balls. Cover and simmer for 15 minutes.

Yield: 30 sausage balls

Holiday Spread

1 cup pecans

2 eggs, hard-boiled

1 medium onion, quartered

1 (4.5 ounce) jar olives

1 cup mayonnaise

½ teaspoon garlic salt

¼ teaspoon cayenne pepper

In food processor, chop together pecans, eggs, onion, and olives. Add remaining ingredients. Blend well. Serve with crackers.

Yield: 3 cups

Stuffed Mushrooms

1 pound large mushrooms

½ cup butter

1 medium onion, chopped

1 cup fine, seasoned bread crumbs

1½ teaspoons salt

¼ teaspoon pepper

½ teaspoon paprika

2 tablespoons ketchup

2 slices bacon, cooked

1 cup sour cream

½ cup milk

Preheat oven to 400 degrees. Wash and dry mushrooms. Remove and chop stems. Melt butter and sauté chopped stems and onions. Stir in crumbs and cook for 2 minutes. Add seasonings and ketchup. Stuff mushroom caps with mixture. Crumble bacon and sprinkle over mushrooms. Place in 11 x 7-inch baking dish. Mix together sour cream and milk. Pour over mushrooms. Sprinkle with additional paprika if desired. Bake for 25 minutes.

Yield: 18 to 24 mushrooms

Reindeer Bites

12 pitted dates

12 cashews

4 strips bacon

Stuff dates with cashews. Cut each strip of bacon crosswise into 3 short portions. Wrap one around each date and secure with toothpick. Fry until done over medium-high heat.

YIELD: 12 SERVINGS

Cucumber Dip

2 medium cucumbers, peeled and grated

1 (8 ounce) package cream cheese, softened

½ teaspoon garlic salt

½ cup green pepper, finely chopped

1 tablespoon hot sauce

Squeeze liquid from cucumbers and save. Beat cream cheese, adding a little cucumber liquid at a time until mixture reaches a good consistency for dipping. Add remaining ingredients and mix well. Stir in grated cucumber. Chill.

Yield: 2½ cups

Stuffed Shrimp

16 large fresh shrimp

¾ cup buttery cracker crumbs

3 tablespoons butter, melted

Clams

2 tablespoons parsley

⅛ teaspoon garlic powder

⅛ teaspoon salt

¼ teaspoon pepper

⅓ cup milk

Preheat oven to 350 degrees. Slit each shrimp along vein side about halfway through. In bowl, combine crumbs and butter. Stir in clams, parsley, garlic powder, salt, and pepper. Stuff each shrimp with clam mixture. Arrange in 11 x 7-inch baking dish. Add milk and bake for 20 minutes.

Yield: 16 shrimp

Clam Dip

1 (8 ounce) container sour cream

¼ cup chili sauce

1 (6.5 ounce) can clams, chopped and drained

¼ cup mayonnaise

1 tablespoon green onion, finely chopped

1 teaspoon lemon juice

In small bowl, combine all ingredients. Mix well. Chill before serving.

Island Christmas Meatballs

1 egg, beaten

¼ cup fine bread crumbs

2 tablespoons fresh cilantro or parsley

2 cloves garlic, minced

⅛ teaspoon ground red pepper

¼ teaspoon salt

1 pound ground beef

¼ cup peanuts, finely chopped

1 (20 ounce) can pineapple chunks, drained

1 (10 ounce) jar sweet-and-sour sauce

Preheat oven to 350 degrees. In medium mixing bowl, combine egg, bread crumbs, cilantro or parsley, garlic, pepper, and salt. Mix well. Add beef and peanuts. Mix well. Shape into 1-inch meatballs. Place in 15 x 10 x 2-inch baking dish. Bake for 20 minutes. Remove from oven and drain. When cool, skewer pineapple chunk and meatball on wooden toothpick. Brush with sweet-and-sour sauce. Bake for 6 minutes. Heat remaining sauce in small saucepan until bubbly. Brush meatballs and fruit again. Display remaining sauce for dipping.

YIELD: 36 MEATBALL SKEWERS

On the second day of Christmas my true love sent to me. . .

Two Beverages a-Blending

It is Christmas in the heart
that puts Christmas in the air.

W. T. ELLIS

Lord Jesus, thank You for all the blessings You rain down on us. Thank You especially for Your living water, given freely that our spiritual thirst might be forever satisfied. Amen.

Let the one who is thirsty come; and let the one who wishes take the free gift of the water of life.

REVELATION 22:17 NIV

Many-Colored Holiday Punch

1 cup sugar

1 cup hot water

1 (12 ounce) can frozen lemonade concentrate, undiluted

1 (46 ounce) can pineapple juice

1 small package unsweetened Kool-Aid (any flavor)

2 liters ginger ale, chilled

Mix sugar and hot water until sugar is dissolved. Combine remaining ingredients except ginger ale. Just before serving, add chilled ginger ale and mix well.

Yield: 25 servings

Wassail

1 gallon apple cider

2 teaspoons whole allspice

2 teaspoons whole cloves

2 cinnamon sticks

⅔ cup sugar

1 orange, sliced

Combine cider, allspice, cloves, cinnamon, and sugar in kettle. Stir well and bring to a boil. Reduce heat, cover, and simmer for 20 minutes. Strain and let cool. Pour into punch bowl. Add orange slices.

Yield: 32 servings

Christmas Eve Cocktail

* * * * * * * * *

2 cups unsweetened pineapple juice

1 cup tomato juice

Juice of 2 lemons

4 mint sprigs

Mix all ingredients except mint and let stand for at least 1 hour. Then chill for 1 hour. Pour into cocktail glasses and garnish with sprig of mint.

YIELD: 4 SERVINGS

Lemonade Cocktail

½ cup sugar

1 cup hot water

1 lemon rind

Juice of 4 large lemons

1 cup cold water

1 lemon, very thinly sliced

Dissolve sugar in hot water. Add lemon rind and let cool. When cool, add lemon juice and cold water. Mix well and strain. Serve in cocktail glasses with ice and lemon slices.

Yield: 4 servings

Banana Punch

16 cups water

4 cups sugar

1 (12 ounce) can frozen orange juice concentrate, undiluted

1 (46 ounce) can pineapple juice

2 drops red food coloring

5 bananas, mashed

2 (32 ounce) bottles ginger ale

Boil 4 cups water with sugar until clear. Add remaining water, orange juice, and pineapple juice. Add food coloring. Stir well. Add bananas. Stir well. Chill. Add ginger ale just before serving.

Yield: 25 servings

Sparkling Harvest Cider

2 quarts apple cider, chilled

1 cup lemon juice

½ cup sugar

1 (32 ounce) bottle ginger ale

6 apple slices

4 cinnamon sticks

In punch bowl, combine cider, lemon juice, and sugar. Stir until sugar dissolves. Just before serving, add ginger ale. Garnish with apple slices and cinnamon sticks. Serve over ice.

Yield: 3 quarts

Granny Nell's Hot Spiced Cider

8 cups apple cider

¼ cup brown sugar, packed

6 cinnamon sticks

1 teaspoon whole allspice

1 teaspoon whole cloves

1 orange, thinly sliced

In saucepan, combine cider and brown sugar. Prepare spice bag by placing cinnamon, allspice, and cloves onto 6-inch square piece of cotton cheese-cloth. Bring corners together and tie with string. Add bag to cider mixture. Bring to a boil. Reduce heat, cover, and simmer for 10 minutes. Remove and discard spice bag. Place cider in mugs and garnish with orange slices.

Yield: 8 servings

Mint Punch

2 cups sugar

4 cups water

2 cups mint leaves

2 cups water

Juice of 6 lemons

2 drops green food coloring

1 liter ginger ale

In saucepan, combine sugar and 4 cups water. Bring to a boil until cooked down into a syrup. In another saucepan, combine mint leaves and 2 cups water. Bring to a boil. Simmer for 5 minutes. Let cool and then pour through strainer. Combine mint water with syrup. Add lemon juice and food coloring. Mix well. Immediately before serving, add ginger ale. Serve in cocktail glasses over crushed ice.

YIELD: 6 SERVINGS

Chocolate Mint Chai Tea

1 tea bag black tea

½ cup boiling water

3 tablespoons sugar

2 tablespoons cocoa powder

2 large candy canes, finely crushed

2 cups milk

1 teaspoon vanilla

1 teaspoon allspice

½ teaspoon cardamom, finely ground

In saucepan, pour boiling water over tea bag. Cover and let stand for 4 minutes. Remove tea bag. Stir in sugar, cocoa, and crushed candy canes. Cook and stir over medium heat until mixture boils. Stir in milk, vanilla, and spices. Heat thoroughly. Do not boil.

YIELD: 4 SERVINGS

Santa's Surprise

1 (46 ounce) can pineapple juice

3 liters lemon-lime soda

2 (6 ounce) cans frozen orange juice concentrate, undiluted

1 (10 ounce) jar maraschino cherries

Chill pineapple juice and lemon-lime soda. Pour 1 liter soda into two ice cube trays. Place maraschino cherry into each cube. Freeze. At serving time, combine pineapple juice and orange juice in punch bowl. Slowly pour in remaining 2 liters soda. Add ice cubes.

YIELD: 30 CUPS

Banana Slurry

4 cups sugar

6 cups water

1 (46 ounce) can pineapple juice

1 (12 ounce) can frozen orange juice concentrate, undiluted

1 (12 ounce) can frozen lemonade concentrate, undiluted

2½ cups water

5 bananas, pureed

6 quarts ginger ale, chilled

Dissolve sugar in water. Add remaining ingredients and mix well. Freeze in 1-quart containers. Remove from freezer and allow to thaw for 45 minutes before serving. Add 1 quart cold ginger ale to each block of punch just before serving.

YIELD: 12 QUARTS

Spice Cups

2½ cups orange juice

1 cup pineapple juice

2 cups water

½ cup sugar

Zest of 1 lemon

1 tablespoon honey

6 whole cloves

½ teaspoon nutmeg, grated

¼ teaspoon allspice

½ teaspoon cinnamon

3 pints ginger ale

Combine juices with water and sugar. Add lemon zest, honey, and spices. Mix and let stand for 3 hours. Strain and add ginger ale. Stir briskly and serve over ice.

Yield: 3 quarts

Minty Grape Cooler

1 cup sugar

1½ cups water

1 cup mint leaves

1 cup lemon juice

2 cups grape juice

28 ounces ginger ale

In saucepan, stir sugar and water over medium heat until sugar dissolves. Cool slightly and pour over mint leaves. Cover and set aside for 1 hour. Strain. Add lemon juice and grape juice. Just before serving, add ginger ale.

YIELD: 2 QUARTS

Danish Coffee

¼ cup chocolate syrup

½ cup ground coffee

2 bay leaves

Zest of 1 orange

3 cups cold water

1 cup whipping cream, whipped

Pour chocolate syrup into coffee pot carafe. Put coffee, bay leaves, and orange zest in basket lined with paper filter. Pour water into coffee maker. Brew as usual. Garnish with whipped cream.

YIELD: 4 SERVINGS

Eggnog

4 eggs, beaten

8 tablespoons sugar

4 cups milk

1 teaspoon vanilla

2 teaspoons nutmeg

Briskly beat eggs and sugar until creamy. Beat in remaining ingredients. Chill until ready to serve.

Yield: 4 servings

Dreamy Holiday Mocha

4 cups milk

4 teaspoons instant coffee

1 (7 ounce) jar marshmallow crème

Whisk together all ingredients until well blended. Heat over medium-low heat until mixture is warmed, stirring constantly. When marshmallow crème is melted, pour into cups and serve.

YIELD: 4 SERVINGS

Coffee Ice Cream Punch

1 gallon strong coffee, brewed and cooled

½ gallon coffee ice cream

1 pint vanilla ice cream

1 pint heavy cream, whipped

½ teaspoon nutmeg

½ teaspoon cinnamon

Blend coffee and half of coffee ice cream to a fairly thick consistency. Chill in punch bowl in refrigerator. When ready to serve, drop in ice cream balls made from remaining coffee ice cream and vanilla ice cream. Top with whipped cream. Sprinkle with nutmeg and cinnamon.

YIELD: 25 SERVINGS

On the third day of Christmas my true love sent to me. . .

Three Breads a-Rising

Christians, awake, salute the happy morn
whereon the Saviour of the world was born.

JOHN BYRON

Dear Jesus, how we long to be nourished by You, the Bread of Life. We are strengthened both physically and spiritually each moment that we spend in Your presence. Amen.

"Very truly I tell you. . .I am the bread of life."

John 6:47–48 niv

Pumpkin Cheese Bread

* * *

2½ cups sugar

1 (8 ounce) package cream cheese, softened

½ cup butter, softened

4 eggs

1 (16 ounce) can pumpkin

3½ cups flour

2 teaspoons baking soda

1 teaspoon salt

½ teaspoon baking powder

1 teaspoon cinnamon

¼ teaspoon ground cloves

1 cup walnuts, chopped

2 cups powdered sugar

3 tablespoons milk

Preheat oven to 350 degrees. Cream together sugar, cream cheese, and butter. Add eggs, one at a time, mixing well after each addition. Blend in pumpkin. Combine flour, baking soda, salt, baking powder, cinnamon, and cloves in separate bowl. Add to pumpkin mixture, stirring just until moistened. Add walnuts. Pour into two greased and floured 9 x 5-inch loaf pans. Bake for 1 hour. Cool for 5 minutes before removing from pans. Combine powdered sugar and milk. Glaze tops.

YIELD: 2 LOAVES

Parmesan Herb Bread

* * *

⅔ cup butter

¼ cup Parmesan cheese, grated

1 large garlic clove, minced

½ teaspoon dried basil

2 (½ pound) loaves French bread, cut in half lengthwise

Combine butter, cheese, garlic, and basil. Spread on cut surfaces of bread. Place on cookie sheet. Broil until lightly browned. Cut into slices.

YIELD: 8 SERVINGS

Mini Christmas Fruitcakes

½ cup light molasses

¼ cup water

1 teaspoon vanilla

1 (15 ounce) package raisins

1 pound candied fruit, chopped

½ cup butter, softened

⅔ cup sugar

3 eggs

1 cup plus 2 tablespoons flour

¼ teaspoon baking soda

1 teaspoon cinnamon

1 teaspoon nutmeg

¼ teaspoon allspice

¼ teaspoon cloves

¼ cup milk

1 cup nuts, chopped

Preheat oven to 325 degrees. In saucepan, combine molasses, water, vanilla, and raisins. Bring to a boil. Reduce heat and simmer for 5 minutes. Remove from heat and stir in candied fruit. Cool. In bowl, cream butter and sugar. Add eggs, one at a time, beating well after each addition. In separate bowl, stir together flour, baking soda, and spices. Add to creamed mixture alternately with milk. Stir in fruit mixture. Stir in nuts. Spoon into paper-lined mini muffin pan, filling each cup two-thirds full. Bake for 24 minutes. Cool. Store in airtight container.

Yield: 6 dozen mini muffins

Pumpkin and Spice Muffins

1 cup flour

½ cup sugar

2 teaspoons baking powder

1½ teaspoons cinnamon

¼ teaspoon ginger

¼ teaspoon nutmeg

½ teaspoon salt

¼ cup butter, cubed

1 cup pumpkin puree

½ cup evaporated milk

1 egg

1½ teaspoons vanilla

⅓ cup raisins

Preheat oven to 400 degrees. Sift together flour, sugar, baking powder, spices, and salt. Cut in butter until fully incorporated. In separate bowl, mix together pumpkin, milk, egg, and vanilla. Pour pumpkin mixture into flour mixture. Add raisins and fold together gently until combined. Pour into greased muffin pan, filling each cup halfway full. Bake for 25 minutes. Cool in pan for 15 minutes. Remove and continue to cool. Store in refrigerator.

Yield: 12 muffins

Nutty Upside-Down Pineapple Muffins

¼ cup brown sugar, packed

2 tablespoons butter, melted

12 pecan halves

1½ cups bran flakes

1 (8 ounce) can crushed pineapple

¼ cup milk

1 egg

¼ cup oil

½ cup pecans, coarsely chopped

1¼ cups flour

3½ teaspoons baking powder

1 teaspoon salt

⅓ cup sugar

Preheat oven to 400 degrees. Cream brown sugar and butter. Using a teaspoon, spoon into greased 12-cup muffin pan. Place pecan half in each. Mix together bran flakes, pineapple, and milk. Let stand for 2 minutes. Beat in egg and oil. Add pecans. Combine remaining dry ingredients. Add to wet mixture and stir. Spoon into muffin cups. Bake for 25 minutes.

YIELD: 12 SERVINGS

Angel Biscuits

1 (.25 ounce) package dry yeast

2 tablespoons warm water

5 cups flour

1 tablespoon plus 1 teaspoon baking powder

¼ cup sugar

1 teaspoon salt

1 teaspoon baking soda

1 cup shortening

2 cups buttermilk

Preheat oven to 400 degrees. Dissolve yeast in water. Sift together dry ingredients. Cut in shortening. Add yeast mixture and buttermilk to dry ingredients. Turn dough out on floured surface and knead lightly. Refrigerate. Roll dough to ½-inch thickness. Cut into rounds with 2-inch biscuit cutter. Fold in half. Place on greased cookie sheet and bake for 20 minutes.

YIELD: 3 DOZEN

Wendy's Sweet Potato Bread

1½ cups sugar

½ cup oil

2 eggs

⅓ cup water

1¾ cups flour

1 teaspoon baking soda

½ teaspoon salt

1 teaspoon nutmeg

1 teaspoon cloves

1½ teaspoons cinnamon

1 cup sweet potatoes, cooked and mashed

½ cup pecans, chopped

½ cup raisins

Preheat oven to 350 degrees. In large bowl, combine sugar, oil, eggs, and water, mixing well. In separate bowl, combine dry ingredients, including spices. Add to egg mixture and mix until moistened. Add remaining ingredients and mix well. Pour into two small greased and floured loaf pans. Bake for 1 hour. Cool for 10 minutes before removing from pans.

YIELD: 2 SMALL LOAVES

Christmas Morning Breakfast Bread

½ cup butter-flavored shortening

⅔ cup brown sugar, packed

2 eggs

3 bananas, sliced

2 cups flour

1 teaspoon baking soda

1 teaspoon baking powder

¾ cup pecans, chopped

1 (6 ounce) package chocolate chips

⅓ cup dates, chopped

⅓ cup maraschino cherries, chopped

Cream shortening and brown sugar in bowl until light and fluffy. Add eggs and bananas. Mix well. Add flour, baking soda, and baking powder. Mix well. Add pecans, chips, and dates. Mix well. Pour into large greased and floured loaf pan. Bake for 35 minutes. Remove from pan and cool. Garnish with cherries. Wrap and allow to sit overnight before cutting.

YIELD: 12 SERVINGS

Merry Muffins

2 cups flour, sifted

½ cup sugar

3 teaspoons baking powder

1 teaspoon salt

1 large egg, beaten

¾ cup milk

⅓ cup oil

⅔ cup chopped walnuts

¼ cup chopped maraschino cherries

¼ cup sweetened cocoa mix

¼ cup powdered sugar

Preheat oven to 400 degrees. Sift together flour, sugar, baking powder, and salt. In separate bowl, combine egg, milk, and oil. Add to flour mixture until moistened. Fold in walnuts. Divide into two portions. Stir cherries into one portion and spoon mixture into one half of each cup of greased 12-cup muffin pan. Stir cocoa mix into remaining batter and fill the other half of each cup. Bake for 20 minutes. Sprinkle with powdered sugar.

Yield: 12 muffins

Aunt Sandy's Blackberry Bread

3 cups flour

2 cups sugar

2½ teaspoons cinnamon

1 teaspoon baking soda

1 teaspoon salt

1 cup vegetable oil

¼ cup milk

4 eggs

2 cups blackberries

Preheat oven to 350 degrees. Sift together dry ingredients in medium mixing bowl, making well in center. Add remaining ingredients and stir until mixture is moistened. Divide batter in half and spoon each half into standard-size greased and floured loaf pan. Bake for 55 minutes.

Yield: 2 loaves

Cheese and Bacon Bread

4 cups flour

½ cup sugar

2 tablespoons baking powder

2 teaspoons salt

2 eggs, beaten

2 cups milk

½ cup vegetable oil

2 cups cheddar cheese, shredded

⅔ cup bacon, cooked and crumbled

Preheat oven to 350 degrees. Grease and flour two 9 x 5-inch loaf pans. In large bowl, combine flour, sugar, baking powder, salt, eggs, milk, and oil. Beat on medium speed for 30 seconds, scraping sides often. Stir in cheese and bacon. Spoon batter into pans. Bake for 45 minutes. Cool for 5 minutes before removing from pans.

Yield: 2 loaves

Holly's Pumpkin Bread

4 eggs

3 cups sugar

1 (16 ounce) can pumpkin

1 cup vegetable oil

3½ cups flour

2 teaspoons baking soda

2 teaspoons salt

1 teaspoon baking powder

1 teaspoon nutmeg

1 teaspoon cinnamon

1 teaspoon allspice

½ teaspoon cloves

⅔ cup water

1 cup pecans

Preheat oven to 350 degrees. In large bowl, beat eggs until thick and foamy. Add sugar, 1 cup at a time, mixing well after each. Mix in pumpkin and oil. Set aside. In separate bowl, combine dry ingredients and mix well. Add dry ingredients to pumpkin mixture, alternating with water. Stir in pecans. Pour into four greased and floured 1-pound coffee cans. Bake for 45 minutes. Cool for 10 minutes before removing from cans.

Yield: 4 medium loaves

Cranberry Tea Loaf

1¼ cups water

¼ cup cranberry juice cocktail

4 regular tea bags

3 cups flour

1 teaspoon baking soda

½ teaspoon salt

1 cup sugar

4 tablespoons butter, softened

2 eggs

1 cup cranberries, chopped

1 cup walnuts or pecans, chopped

Preheat oven to 350 degrees. In small saucepan, bring water and cranberry juice to a boil. Add tea bags. Cover and brew for 5 minutes. Cool. In small bowl, combine flour, baking soda, and salt. In large mixing bowl, beat sugar and butter until well blended. Beat in eggs, one at a time. Beat in cooled tea mixture. Gradually beat in flour mixture until blended. Stir in cranberries and nuts. Pour into greased 9 x 5-inch loaf pan. Bake for 75 minutes. Cool for 10 minutes before removing from pan.

YIELD: 8 SERVINGS

Honey Lemon Mini Loaves

½ cup butter, softened

1 cup sugar

2 eggs

1 teaspoon vanilla

5 teaspoons lemon zest

¼ cup honey

½ cup sour cream

1½ cups flour

1 teaspoon baking powder

¼ teaspoon baking soda

¼ teaspoon salt

3 tablespoons milk

¼ cup lemon juice

½ cup sugar

Preheat oven to 350 degrees. In large bowl, cream butter and sugar until fluffy. Stir in eggs, vanilla, lemon zest, honey, and sour cream. Mix well. Incorporate all dry ingredients just until combined. Stir in milk. Spoon batter into greased mini loaf pans. Bake for 15 to 20 minutes. Cool for 15 minutes. Remove from pans. Mix together lemon juice and sugar in small pan. Stir over low heat until sugar dissolves. Spoon over hot loaves. Cool completely before storing in airtight containers.

YIELD: 8 MINI LOAVES

Honey Tea Ring

1 (8 ounce) package cream cheese, softened

¼ cup sugar

½ teaspoon vanilla

2 ½ cups baking mix

⅓ cup chopped nuts

⅓ cup raisins

2 tablespoons honey

Preheat oven to 425 degrees. Cream together cream cheese, sugar, and vanilla. Prepare baking mix as instructed for rolled biscuits. Place on lightly floured surface and roll out to 18 x 12-inch rectangle. Spread with cream cheese mixture. Sprinkle with nuts and raisins. Roll up, starting on long side. Seal long edge. Place on greased cookie sheet. Join ends to form ring. Cut three-quarters of the way through ring at 1-inch intervals. Lay each cut section on its side. Bake for 15 minutes. Brush top with honey. Bake for another 6 minutes. Brush with honey again.

YIELD: 10 SERVINGS

Date Nut Bread

3 cups flour

¼ cup sugar

¼ cup brown sugar

1 teaspoon salt

6 teaspoons baking powder

1½ cups milk

1 egg, beaten

3 tablespoons butter, melted

1 cup nuts, chopped

1 cup dates, chopped

Preheat oven to 375 degrees. In medium bowl, combine flour, sugars, salt, and baking powder. In small bowl, mix together milk and egg. Add to flour mixture. Add butter. Mix well. Add nuts and dates. Stir until well blended. Bake in large greased loaf pan for 1 hour.

YIELD: 1 LARGE LOAF

Holiday Spice Bread

1 cup milk

½ cup butter

1 teaspoon salt

½ cup sugar

2 (.25 ounce) packages dry yeast

¼ cup lukewarm water

4 eggs, beaten

1 teaspoon lemon zest

4½ cups flour

1 teaspoon ground aniseed

¼ teaspoon nutmeg

2 tablespoons butter, melted

Preheat oven to 325 degrees. In small saucepan, scald milk. Add butter, salt, and sugar. Stir well. Remove from heat and cool. In large bowl, dissolve yeast in lukewarm water. Add eggs and lemon zest. Pour in milk mixture. Combine flour with aniseed and nutmeg. Stir into milk mixture. On lightly floured surface, knead dough well. Cover lightly with cloth and let rise for 3 hours in warm area until doubled in size. Grease 32 muffin cups. Fill each half full with dough. Brush tops with butter. Let rise for 30 minutes. Bake for 20 minutes. Remove from pan immediately.

Yield: 32 servings

Blueberry Quick Bread

2½ cups flour

¾ cup sugar

1 tablespoon baking powder

½ teaspoon salt

6 tablespoons butter

¾ cup walnuts, chopped

2 eggs

1 cup milk

1 teaspoon vanilla

1½ cups blueberries

Preheat oven to 350 degrees. In large bowl, combine flour, sugar, baking powder, and salt. Cut in butter. Stir in walnuts. In small bowl, beat eggs slightly. Stir in milk and vanilla. Stir egg mixture into flour mixture until moistened. Gently stir blueberries into batter. Spoon evenly into greased and floured 9 x 5-inch loaf pan. Bake for 1 hour and 20 minutes. Cool in pan for 10 minutes. Serve warm and refrigerate remaining bread.

YIELD: 1 LARGE LOAF

Cranberry Muffins

1¾ cups flour

¼ cup sugar

2½ teaspoons baking powder

¾ teaspoon salt

1 egg, well beaten

¾ cup milk

⅓ cup coconut oil

1 (8 ounce) can jellied cranberry sauce, cubed

Preheat oven to 400 degrees. Combine flour, sugar, baking powder, and salt. Make a well in center. Combine egg, milk, and oil in separate bowl. Pour into well of dry ingredients. Mix enough to moisten. Fill 12 greased muffin cups halfway full. Add 2 to 3 cranberry sauce cubes to each. Spoon in remaining batter. Bake for 25 minutes.

YIELD: 12 MUFFINS

On the fourth day of Christmas my true love sent to me. . .

Four Breakfast Dishes a-Baking

Blest Christmas morn,
though murky clouds pursue the way,
thy light was born
where storm enshrouds not dawn nor day!

Mary Baker Eddy

Dear Father, how grateful we are for Your mercies that are new every morning. Each day brings with it a special joy, knowing that You have called us Your sons and daughters. Amen.

In the morning, Lord, you hear my voice; in the morning I lay my requests before you and wait expectantly.

Psalm 5:3 niv

Christmas Morning Casserole

½ pound bacon

½ cup onion, chopped

½ cup green pepper, chopped

12 eggs

1 cup milk

1 (16 ounce) package frozen hash brown potatoes, thawed

4 ounces cheddar cheese, shredded

1 teaspoon salt

½ teaspoon pepper

¼ teaspoon dill weed

Preheat oven to 350 degrees. Fry bacon until crisp. Crumble and set aside. Using bacon drippings, sauté onion and green pepper until tender. In large bowl, beat eggs and milk together. Add hash browns, cheese, salt, pepper, dill, onion, green pepper, and bacon. Stir. Pour into greased 13 x 9-inch baking dish. Bake uncovered for 35 to 45 minutes.

Yield: 6 to 8 servings

Cinnamon Raisin French Toast

2 eggs, slightly beaten

½ cup milk

½ teaspoon cinnamon

8 slices raisin bread

1 (8 ounce) package cream cheese

½ cup maple syrup

Beat eggs, milk, and cinnamon together and set aside. Spread cream cheese on raisin bread and press two pieces together. Dip in egg mixture, coating both sides. Fry in lightly greased pan or on griddle. Serve with syrup.

Yield: 4 servings

Poached Eggs and Tomatoes

½ cup onion, finely chopped

1 (16 ounce) can Italian-seasoned tomatoes

½ teaspoon salt

¼ teaspoon pepper

1 tablespoon butter

2 tablespoons flour

1 cup milk

1 cup cheddar cheese, shredded

¼ teaspoon paprika

8 eggs

2 tablespoons soft bread crumbs

1 tablespoon butter, melted

3 slices bacon, cooked and diced

Sauté onions until tender. Stir in tomatoes, salt, and pepper. Cook, stirring, about 10 minutes. Add butter. Once butter is melted, remove from heat and stir in flour. Add milk. Return to heat and bring to a boil, stirring constantly. Add ⅓ cup cheese and paprika. Continue cooking, stirring constantly, until cheese is melted. Remove from heat. In skillet, bring 1 inch of water to a boil. Reduce heat to simmer. Break each egg into a saucer before slipping into water. Cook, covered, for 3 to 5 minutes. Lift out of water with slotted spoon. Drain on paper towel. Pour tomato mixture into 1½-quart baking dish. Arrange eggs on top of sauce. Sprinkle ⅓ cup cheese over eggs. Toss crumbs in butter and sprinkle on top. Add remaining ⅓ cup cheese and bacon. Brown under boiler.

YIELD: 4 TO 6 SERVINGS

Broccoli on Toast

1 bunch broccoli

6 slices toast, buttered

4 tablespoons butter

4 tablespoons flour

½ teaspoon salt

¼ teaspoon pepper

2 cups milk

1 teaspoon onion, finely chopped

2 hard-boiled eggs, minced

Wash broccoli and cook in salted water until tender. Drain. Set aside. Place buttered toast in bottom of buttered baking dish. Arrange broccoli on top of toast. In saucepan, melt butter and add flour, salt, and pepper. Blend thoroughly and stir until mixture begins to clump. Slowly add milk and stir constantly until sauce is smooth. Cover and cook without stirring on low heat for 20 minutes. Add onion and eggs. Pour over toast and broccoli.

YIELD: 6 SERVINGS

Bacon and Eggs Casserole

18 slices bacon

¾ cup butter

12 slices bread

6 slices American cheese

6 eggs

3 cups milk

½ teaspoon salt

Butter 13 x 9-inch pan. Fry bacon and break into pieces. Set aside. Butter both sides of bread. Cut off crusts. Place 6 slices in bottom of pan. Cover each with cheese and bacon. Lay remaining slices of bread on top. Beat together eggs, milk, and salt. Pour over bread. Let stand in refrigerator overnight. Bake at 325 degrees for 1 hour.

YIELD: 12 TO 16 SERVINGS

Potato Pancakes

4 medium baking potatoes

2 tablespoons fresh chives, chopped

2 teaspoons salt

1 teaspoon black pepper

3 tablespoons butter

3 tablespoons oil

Peel and grate potatoes into large mixing bowl. Do not drain. Add chives, salt, and pepper. Mix well. Heat some of the butter and oil in large skillet over high heat. Use 2 tablespoons of mixture for each pancake. Over medium heat, fry 3 to 4 at a time, flattening with spatula. Pancakes should be about 3 inches in diameter. Fry for 2 to 3 minutes on each side or until crisp and golden. Add more butter and oil after each batch.

YIELD: 4 SERVINGS

Cheese and Sausage Strata

½ pound pork sausage, crumbled

1 cup mushrooms, sliced

2 cups cheese, shredded

4 cups sourdough or Italian bread
cubes

¼ cup green onions, sliced

1 cup milk

5 eggs, beaten

Preheat oven to 350 degrees. Brown sausage and mushrooms. Drain. Stir in cheese, bread cubes, and onions. Spoon into greased 12 x 8-inch baking dish. Beat milk and eggs. Pour over sausage mixture. Cover. Refrigerate overnight. Bake uncovered for 45 minutes. Let stand for 10 minutes before serving.

Yield: 6 servings

Asparagus Quiche

1 (9 inch) unbaked pie shell

1 egg white, beaten

1 pound fresh asparagus, trimmed

4 slices bacon, cooked and crumbled

2 cups Swiss cheese, shredded

4 eggs

1½ cups light cream

¼ teaspoon salt

⅛ teaspoon nutmeg

⅛ teaspoon black pepper

Preheat oven to 375 degrees. Brush pie shell with egg white and set aside. Cut asparagus into ½-inch pieces and boil in salted water for 5 minutes. Drain. Sprinkle bacon over bottom of pie shell. Sprinkle cheese over bacon. Beat eggs with cream, salt, nutmeg, and pepper just until combined. Sprinkle asparagus pieces over cheese. Pour egg mixture into pie shell. Bake on lower rack for 40 minutes. Cool for 10 minutes.

Yield: 8 servings

Breakfast Casserole

2 pounds pork sausage

12 eggs

2 cups milk

2 teaspoons salt

2 teaspoons dry mustard

12 slices day-old white bread, cubed

2 cups cheddar cheese, shredded

Preheat oven to 350 degrees. Brown sausage and drain well. Beat eggs, milk, salt, and mustard in blender. Pour egg mixture over bread cubes in greased 14 x 9-inch baking dish. Add sausage. Cover with cheese. Bake for 1 hour.

YIELD: 16 SERVINGS

Ham and Cheese French Toast

3 eggs

¾ cup milk

1 tablespoon sugar

¼ teaspoon salt

8 slices white bread, lightly buttered

4 slices ham

4 slices Swiss or American cheese

2 tablespoons butter

Beat together eggs and milk. Add sugar and salt. Make 4 sandwiches with bread, ham, and cheese. Cut into quarters diagonally. Place in single layer in shallow baking dish. Pour egg mixture over sandwiches, covering completely. Refrigerate overnight. Just before serving, melt butter in skillet. Sauté sandwiches until golden brown on both sides and cheese is melted.

YIELD: 4 SERVINGS

Apple Fritters

1 cup flour

1½ teaspoons baking powder

½ teaspoon salt

2 tablespoons sugar

1 egg, beaten

½ cup plus 1 tablespoon milk

1½ cups apples, finely chopped

3 tablespoons powdered sugar, sifted

Sift together flour, baking powder, salt, and sugar. Combine egg and milk. Pour into dry ingredients and stir until smooth. Fold in apples and drop tablespoonfuls of mixture into hot oil. Fry until brown. Roll in powdered sugar. Repeat until batter is used up.

Yield: 18 servings

Ham Muffins

1 cup flour

2 teaspoons baking powder

1 teaspoon sugar

1 teaspoon salt

¼ cup cornmeal

2 eggs

¼ cup oil

¾ cup milk

1 cup ground cooked ham

Preheat oven to 400 degrees. Grease 8 muffin-pan cups. In medium bowl, sift together flour, baking powder, sugar, and salt. Add cornmeal. Mix well. In separate bowl, beat together eggs, oil, and milk. Add flour mixture and ham, stirring only until moistened. Spoon into prepared cups. Bake for 18 minutes.

YIELD: 8 MUFFINS

Sausage Scramble

1 pound sausage

6 eggs, slightly beaten

½ cup milk

½ teaspoon salt

¼ teaspoon pepper

6 slices toast, buttered

Brown sausage in skillet. Pour off some of the fat. In bowl, combine eggs, milk, salt, and pepper. Stir lightly with fork until egg is well blended. Add to sausage. Cook until creamy. Serve on toast.

Yield: 6 servings

Eggs Royale

2 cups seasoned croutons

1 cup cheddar cheese, shredded

4 eggs, slightly beaten

2 cups milk

½ teaspoon salt

½ teaspoon dry mustard

⅛ teaspoon onion powder

½ teaspoon pepper

10 slices bacon, cooked and crumbled

Preheat oven to 325 degrees. Combine croutons and cheese. Put in bottom of greased 2-quart casserole dish. Mix together eggs, milk, salt, mustard, onion powder, and pepper until well blended. Pour over croutons and cheese. Sprinkle bacon on top. Bake for 1 hour.

Yield: 6 servings

Five Candies a-Boiling

The children were nestled all snug in their beds,
while visions of sugar-plums danced in their heads.

CLEMENT C. MOORE, *The Night Before Christmas*

Wonderful Father, the sweetness of Your presence brings joy to our hearts and a song to our lips. Thank You for the sweetest of gifts—Your Son, Jesus. Amen.

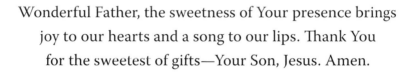

How sweet your words taste to me;
they are sweeter than honey.

Psalm 119:103 nlt

Harvest Popcorn

2 quarts freshly popped popcorn, unsalted

3 cups shoestring potatoes

1 cup salted mixed nuts

¼ cup butter, melted

1 teaspoon dill weed

1 teaspoon Worcestershire sauce

½ teaspoon lemon-pepper seasoning

¼ teaspoon garlic powder

¼ teaspoon onion

Preheat oven to 325 degrees. Combine popcorn, shoestring potatoes, and nuts in large roasting pan. Set aside. Combine remaining ingredients and mix well. Pour over popcorn. Stir lightly. Bake for 10 minutes. Stir lightly. Cool completely. Store in airtight container.

YIELD: 2½ QUARTS

Granny Bill's Peanut Patties

3 cups sugar

3 cups raw peanuts

1 cup corn syrup

½ cup water

½ cup butter

1 tablespoon vanilla

3 drops red food coloring

In saucepan, cook sugar, peanuts, corn syrup, and water for 7 minutes without stirring. Remove from heat and add butter, vanilla, and food coloring. Stir constantly for 6 minutes or until creamy. Pour in portions onto greased cookie sheet. How much depends on desired patty size. Cool. Store in airtight container.

YIELD: SEVERAL DOZEN PATTIES

Daddy Park's Divinity

2 cups sugar

½ cup hot water

½ cup corn syrup

Dash of salt

2 jumbo egg whites

1½ tablespoons vanilla

1 cup pecans, chopped

Place sugar in medium saucepan. In measuring cup, combine water, corn syrup, and salt and add to saucepan. Stir slightly. Boil until syrup reaches 300 to 310 degrees on candy thermometer. While waiting for right temperature, beat egg whites to soft peaks. When syrup reaches right temperature, pour slowly over egg whites. Beat until mixture loses its shine. Add vanilla and continue beating. Add pecans and stir. Spoon quickly onto wax paper, making small mounds. Cool. Store in airtight container.

YIELD: 2 DOZEN CANDIES

Sandra's Frosted Pecans

1 egg white

1 tablespoon cold water

2 cups pecans

1 cup sugar

1 teaspoon cinnamon

¼ teaspoon allspice

¼ teaspoon cloves

¼ teaspoon nutmeg

1 teaspoon salt

Preheat oven to 225 degrees. Beat egg white with cold water until frothy. Stir in pecans. Add sugar, spices, and salt. Mix well. Pour onto cookie sheet covered with parchment paper. Bake for 45 to 60 minutes, stirring occasionally. Cool. Store in airtight container.

Yield: 2 cups

Yum Yum Peanuts

1 cup chocolate chips

2 cups butterscotch chips

2 ounces paraffin

2 cups cocktail peanuts

Melt together chips and paraffin in double boiler, stirring constantly. Add peanuts. Drop teaspoonfuls onto wax paper. Cool completely. Store in airtight container.

YIELD: 2 CUPS

Hazelnut Rounds

½ cup shortening

⅓ cup butter

2½ cups flour

1¼ cups brown sugar, packed

1 egg

1 teaspoon vanilla

½ teaspoon baking soda

¼ teaspoon salt

1¼ cups hazelnuts, toasted and ground

1 cup milk chocolate chips, melted

Cream together shortening and butter in large bowl. Add 1 cup flour and mix well. Add brown sugar, egg, vanilla, baking soda, and salt. Mix well. Stir in remaining 1½ cups flour and ¾ cup nuts. Shape dough into two 10-inch rolls. Wrap in wax paper and chill for 4 hours. Preheat oven to 375 degrees. Remove rolls from refrigerator and cut into ¼-inch-thick slices. Place 1 inch apart on ungreased cookie sheet. Bake for 10 minutes. Remove from oven and cool. Drizzle with chocolate and sprinkle with remaining ½ cup nuts.

YIELD: 5 DOZEN COOKIES

Aunt Mick's Peanut Brittle

---

1 cup sugar

½ cup corn syrup

½ cup water

1 cup raw peanuts

½ teaspoon vanilla

1 teaspoon baking soda

Combine sugar, syrup, and water in saucepan. Boil until syrup reaches 235 to 240 degrees on candy thermometer. Add peanuts. Continue boiling until syrup is light brown in color and reaches 300 to 310 degrees. Remove from heat. Add vanilla and baking soda. Mix well. Pour onto wax paper–lined cookie sheet, spreading as thin as possible. When nearly cool, wet hands in cold water and turn candy over, stretching to desired thinness.

YIELD: 48 PIECES

Sour Cream Fudge

2 cups sugar

2 tablespoons light corn syrup

2 tablespoons butter

1 cup sour cream

1 teaspoon vanilla

¾ cup pecans, chopped

In medium saucepan, combine sugar, corn syrup, butter, and sour cream. Cook on medium-high heat until candy thermometer reads 234 to 240 degrees, stirring constantly. Allow mixture to cool. Add vanilla and beat until smooth. Add pecans and mix well. Pour into 11 x 9-inch baking pan. Allow to set before slicing into squares.

YIELD: 24 SERVINGS

Red Hot Popcorn

1 cup Red Hots candies

1 cup sugar

½ cup butter

½ cup light corn syrup

6 to 7 quarts popped popcorn

Preheat oven to 250 degrees. In saucepan, combine candies, sugar, butter, and corn syrup. Bring to a boil, stirring constantly. Continue boiling for 5 minutes without stirring. Pour popcorn onto large buttered jelly roll pan. Pour candy mixture over popcorn and stir to coat as completely as possible. Bake for 1 hour, stirring every 15 minutes. Cool completely. Store in airtight container.

YIELD: 6 QUARTS

Noel Fudge

2 cups sugar

¾ cup milk

1 teaspoon corn syrup

2 tablespoons butter

1 teaspoon vanilla

1 cup red and green candied cherries, diced

½ cup nuts

In saucepan, bring sugar, milk, and corn syrup to a boil. Simmer for 8 minutes or to 242 to 248 degrees on candy thermometer. Remove from heat and stir in butter and vanilla. Cool. Beat with spoon until mixture loses its glossiness. Stir in fruit and nuts. Pour into buttered 9-inch square pan. Allow to cool completely. Cut into squares.

YIELD: 16 SQUARES

Sandy's Caramel Corn

½ cup butter

1 cup brown sugar, packed

¼ cup light corn syrup

½ teaspoon salt

¼ teaspoon baking soda

1 teaspoon vanilla

3 quarts popped popcorn

Preheat oven to 250 degrees. In medium saucepan, combine butter, brown sugar, corn syrup, and salt. Bring to a boil, stirring constantly. Continue boiling for 5 minutes without stirring. Remove from heat and add baking soda and vanilla. Pour popcorn onto large buttered jelly roll pan. Pour caramel mixture over popcorn and stir to coat as completely as possible. Bake for 1 hour, stirring every 15 minutes. Cool completely. Store in airtight container.

Yield: 3 quarts

Aunt Lisa's Pecan Pralines

1 cup sugar

1 cup light brown sugar

½ cup light cream

1½ cups pecan halves

3 tablespoons butter

In large, heavy saucepan, combine sugars and cream. Over medium heat, bring to a boil, stirring with wooden spoon. Continue stirring until mixture reaches 228 degrees on candy thermometer. Add pecans and butter. Cook over medium heat, stirring frequently until mixture reaches 236 degrees. Cool for 10 minutes. Stir for 1 minute. Drop tablespoonfuls 3 inches apart onto foil or wax paper.

YIELD: 1 DOZEN PRALINE CANDIES

Granny C's Crazy Crunch

2 quarts popped popcorn

1⅓ cups nuts

1⅓ cups sugar

1 cup butter

½ cup corn syrup

1 teaspoon vanilla

Spread out popcorn and nuts on buttered jelly roll pan. In medium saucepan, combine sugar, butter, and corn syrup. Bring to a boil over medium heat, stirring constantly. Boil, stirring occasionally, for 10 to 15 minutes or until mixture is light caramel color. Remove from heat. Stir in vanilla. Pour over popcorn and nuts. Mix to coat. Spread to dry. Break apart and store in airtight container.

Yield: 2 pounds

GORP

2 cups corn-and-rice cereal

2 cups toasted O-shaped cereal

2 cups cheese-flavored snack crackers

2 cups mini pretzel twists

1 cup raisins

1 cup sweetened dried cranberries

1 cup dry-roasted salted peanuts

1 cup sunflower seeds

1 cup candy-coated chocolate pieces

1 cup mini marshmallows

Combine all ingredients in large airtight container. Mix well. Store at room temperature.

Yield: 12 (1-cup) servings

Dark Chocolate Fudge

½ cup light corn syrup

⅓ cup evaporated milk

3 cups semisweet chocolate chips

¾ cup powdered sugar

2 teaspoons vanilla

1 cup nuts, coarsely chopped

Line 8-inch square baking pan with parchment paper. In saucepan, combine syrup and milk. Stir well. Stir in chocolate chips until melted. Add sugar, vanilla, and nuts. Remove from heat. Using wooden spoon, beat until thick and glossy. Spread in pan. Refrigerate for 2 hours.

YIELD: 9 SERVINGS

Party Taffy

2 cups brown sugar, firmly packed

½ cup sugar

1 tablespoon butter

⅓ cup water

2 tablespoons cider vinegar

In large saucepan, combine all ingredients. Cook over low heat, stirring only until sugar dissolves. Remove any crystals around edge. Continue cooking over medium-high heat, without stirring, to 275 degrees on candy thermometer. Pour onto large buttered jelly roll pan. Let cool until semi-firm. Butter hands and rub them with cornstarch. Pull until taffy is light colored and porous. Twist into ropes and place on pan. Cut with scissors or break apart.

Yield: 10 servings

Minted Pecans

1 cup water

½ cup sugar

¼ teaspoon mint oil

1 cup marshmallow crème

3 cups toasted pecans

Preheat oven to 250 degrees. Boil water and sugar until mixture spins a thread at 230 to 234 degrees. Add mint oil, marshmallow crème, and pecans. Stir to coat well. Place on wax paper and separate. Toast pecans in oven for 35 minutes.

YIELD: 3 CUPS

Pecan Chews

1 cup sugar

½ cup brown sugar

⅔ cup light corn syrup

1¼ cups evaporated milk

⅓ cup water

½ cup butter, softened

⅛ teaspoon baking soda

2¾ cups pecans

⅛ teaspoon salt

In large saucepan, combine sugars, corn syrup, milk, water, butter, and baking soda. Bring to a boil, stirring constantly. Bring to 242 to 248 degrees on candy thermometer. Remove from heat and add pecans and salt. Pour into buttered 8-inch square pan. Let set for 2 hours before cutting into squares.

YIELD: 9 SQUARES

Cathedral Windows

1 (12 ounce) package chocolate
   chips

½ cup butter

1 (10.5 ounce) bag colored mini
   marshmallows

1 cup pecans, finely chopped

¼ cup powdered sugar, sifted

Melt chocolate chips and butter in double boiler. Cool slightly and pour over marshmallows and pecans. Mix well. Divide in half on wax paper and sprinkle with powdered sugar. Shape into two rolls. Refrigerate. Cool completely before slicing. Keep refrigerated.

YIELD: 6 SERVINGS

Honey Crunch

3 cups corn bran cereal

1 cup quick oats

1 cup coarsely chopped nuts

1 teaspoon cinnamon

¼ teaspoon salt

½ cup butter

⅓ cup honey

¼ cup brown sugar, firmly packed

½ cup raisins

Preheat oven to 325 degrees. In large bowl, combine cereal, oats, nuts, cinnamon, and salt. In small saucepan, combine butter, honey, and brown sugar. Cook over low heat, stirring constantly, until sugar is melted and ingredients are well blended. Pour over cereal mixture. Mix until well coated. Spread evenly into 15 x 10-inch jelly roll pan. Bake for 25 minutes, stirring occasionally. Immediately remove from heat and add raisins. Spread mixture on wax paper. Cool completely. Store in airtight container.

YIELD: 7 CUPS

Six Cookies a-Cooling

The best of all gifts around any Christmas tree:
the presence of a happy family all wrapped up in each other.

Burton Hillis

Lord Jesus, thank You for this special time to celebrate Your birth here on earth. As we gather during this Christmas season with our earthly family, we are thankful for the sacrifice You made for us. Together we will sing joyful praises to Your Name. Amen.

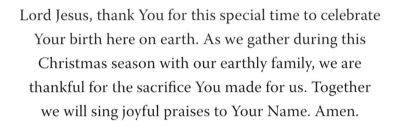

God was very kind to us because of the Son he dearly loves, and so we should praise God.

EPHESIANS 1:6 CEV

Swedish Yuletide Cookies

½ cup butter

⅓ cup sugar

½ teaspoon vanilla

1 egg yolk

1¼ cups flour

½ teaspoon baking powder

¼ teaspoon salt

1 egg white, slightly beaten

½ cup walnuts or pecans

2 tablespoons sugar

Cream together butter, sugar, vanilla, and egg yolk. Combine flour, baking powder, and salt in separate bowl. Blend into creamed mixture. Chill dough for 1 hour. Roll thin. Brush with beaten egg white. Cut into 2½-inch squares. Place on lightly greased baking sheet. Cut each corner diagonally almost to center. Mix nuts and sugar together. Center a small spoonful on each square. Fold corners together. Bake for 15 to 18 minutes. Cool.

YIELD: 2 DOZEN COOKIES

Christmas Amaretti

½ cup sugar

½ cup powdered sugar

¼ cup flour

⅛ teaspoon salt

1 (8 ounce) can almond paste

2 egg whites

½ cup almonds, blanched and finely chopped

1 cup green and red candied cherries, halved

Preheat oven to 300 degrees. Sift both sugars with flour and salt; set aside. Using a fork, break almond paste into small pieces in medium bowl. Add egg whites. Beat with electric mixer at medium speed until blended. Roll teaspoonfuls of dough into balls and then roll in almonds. Lightly flatten into rounds and press halves of candied cherries on top. Place 2 inches apart on lightly greased cookie sheets. Bake for 20 to 25 minutes. Cool and store in airtight container.

YIELD: 2½ DOZEN COOKIES

Gingerbread Men

½ cup sugar

½ cup light molasses

½ cup butter, softened

1 large egg

2½ cups flour

1½ teaspoons ginger

1 teaspoon cinnamon

½ teaspoon ground cloves

½ teaspoon baking powder

¼ teaspoon salt

1 cup powdered sugar

1½ tablespoons milk

1 teaspoon vanilla

Raisins

In large bowl, beat sugar, molasses, butter, and egg until fluffy. Add flour, spices, baking powder, and salt. Mix until smooth. Roll into ball, wrap, and refrigerate for 30 minutes. Roll out dough to ⅛-inch thickness. Using a 6-inch cookie cutter, cut out gingerbread men. Bake for 12 to 15 minutes. While cooling, combine powdered sugar, milk, and vanilla. Use icing and raisins to decorate.

Yield: 12 to 14 cookies

Holiday Macaroons

2 eggs

¾ cup sugar

⅓ cup flour

¼ teaspoon baking powder

⅛ teaspoon salt

1 tablespoon butter, melted

1 teaspoon vanilla

2½ cups flaked coconut

¼ teaspoon cinnamon

½ teaspoon lemon zest

Preheat oven to 325 degrees. In small bowl, beat eggs until foamy. Gradually add sugar, beating until thick and lemon colored. Fold in flour, baking powder, and salt. Add butter, vanilla, and coconut. Mix well. Divide batter in half. Add cinnamon to one half, lemon peel to the other. Drop teaspoonfuls onto lightly greased and floured cookie sheets. Bake for 12 to 15 minutes. Let stand for 2 minutes before removing to rack. Store in airtight container when cool.

YIELD: 3 DOZEN COOKIES

Candied Fudgies

½ cup butter

4 (1 ounce) squares unsweetened chocolate

2 cups sugar

1¼ cups flour

2 teaspoons cinnamon

½ teaspoon salt

4 eggs, beaten

1 teaspoon vanilla

1½ cups red and green candied cherries, halved

1 cup walnuts, chopped

Preheat oven to 350 degrees. In saucepan, melt butter and chocolate over low heat. Cool for 10 minutes. Combine sugar, flour, cinnamon, and salt. Stir eggs and vanilla into cooled chocolate mixture until smooth. Fold in cherries and walnuts, reserving ¼ cup of each. Transfer to greased 13 x 9-inch baking pan. Arrange remaining cherries and walnuts on top. Bake for 35 minutes. Cool. Cut into bars.

Yield: 2 dozen cookies

Christmas Chewies

1 (14 ounce) can sweetened condensed milk

1 pound dates, chopped

2 (3.5 ounce) cans or 2⅔ cups flaked coconut

2½ cups pecans, chopped

½ teaspoon salt

1 teaspoon vanilla

Preheat oven to 325 degrees. In large bowl, mix together all ingredients. Drop teaspoonfuls onto ungreased cookie sheet. Bake for 20 minutes or until lightly browned.

Yield: 2½ dozen cookies

Santa Claus Cookies

3 cups flour

1½ teaspoons cinnamon

1 teaspoon cloves

1 teaspoon ginger

⅛ teaspoon baking powder

⅛ teaspoon salt

1 cup butter, softened

1¼ cups light brown sugar, packed

1 egg

½ cup almonds, blanched and sliced

Preheat oven to 350 degrees. Sift flour with spices, baking powder, and salt. Set aside. Beat butter, brown sugar, and egg at high speed until light and fluffy. Stir in flour mixture and almonds, mixing with hands. Refrigerate dough, covered, for 2 hours. Remove one-quarter of dough from refrigerator at a time. With hands, flatten dough to make 4-inch rectangle. Roll out dough to 9 x 5-inch rectangle. Cut out dough using 5-inch Santa cutter. Place on lightly greased cookie sheets. Repeat until all dough is gone. Bake for 20 to 25 minutes. Remove from pan and cool. Decorate as desired.

YIELD: 14 TO 15 COOKIES

Jingle Bell Jumbles

1 egg

2 tablespoons instant coffee

½ teaspoon vanilla

½ cup butter

½ cup granulated sugar

¼ cup brown sugar, firmly packed

1 cup flour

1 teaspoon baking soda

¼ teaspoon salt

3 squares semisweet baking chocolate, chopped

3 squares white chocolate, chopped

2 cups nuts (pecans, walnuts, or macadamia)

1 cup dried cherries

Preheat oven to 350 degrees. In small bowl, combine egg, coffee, and vanilla. Mix well and set aside. In large bowl, cream butter and sugar with electric mixer until fluffy. Add flour, baking soda, and salt and mix until well blended. Stir in chocolate, nuts, and cherries. Drop tablespoonfuls onto ungreased cookie sheet. Bake for 10 to 12 minutes. Cool for 2 minutes before removing from pan.

YIELD: 3 DOZEN COOKIES

Orange Candy Cookies

3 cups shortening

1½ cups sugar

3 cups packed brown sugar

5 eggs

4½ cups flour

2¼ cups rolled oats

2¼ teaspoons baking powder

2¼ teaspoons baking soda

¼ cup water

2 (8 ounce) packages orange slice candy, chopped

3 cups coconut, flaked

2¼ cups pecans, chopped

Preheat oven to 325 degrees. Cream shortening and sugars with electric mixer until fluffy. Add eggs, flour, oats, baking powder, baking soda, and water. Using wooden spoon, blend well. Stir in candy, coconut, and pecans. Drop teaspoonfuls onto ungreased cookie sheet. Bake for 12 minutes or until brown. Cool completely.

YIELD: 20 DOZEN COOKIES

Vera's Coconut Cookies

½ cup butter

2 cups vanilla wafer crumbs

1 cup chocolate chips

½ cup pecans, chopped

1 cup coconut, flaked

1 can sweetened condensed milk

Preheat oven to 350 degrees. Melt butter in 8-inch square baking pan. Sprinkle evenly with wafer crumbs. Sprinkle with chocolate chips and nuts. Top with coconut. Pour milk over all. Bake for 30 minutes. When cool, cut into squares.

YIELD: 9 COOKIES

Delicate Almond Cookies

1 cup butter, melted

1 cup vegetable oil

1 cup creamy peanut butter

2 cups sugar

4 cups flour

1½ tablespoons water

1 teaspoon baking powder

½ teaspoon baking soda

1 egg, beaten

1 tablespoon almond extract

Preheat oven to 300 degrees. Combine butter, oil, and peanut butter. Cream in sugar. Add flour and stir. In separate bowl, combine water, baking powder, baking soda, egg, and almond extract. Mix well and pour into middle of flour mixture. Stir well. Roll into teaspoon-size balls and place on ungreased cookie sheet. Bake for 20 minutes. Cool. Store in airtight container.

YIELD: 8 DOZEN COOKIES

Date Whirls

2 cups dates, chopped

1 cup sugar

1 cup water

1 cup nuts, chopped

1 cup shortening

2 cups brown sugar, firmly packed

3 eggs

4 cups flour

1 teaspoon salt

⅓ teaspoon baking soda

In saucepan, combine dates, sugar, and water. Cook over low heat, stirring frequently for 10 minutes. Cool and add nuts. Blend together shortening and brown sugar. Beat in eggs. Sift together flour, salt, and soda. Stir into shortening mixture and mix well. Refrigerate for 1 hour. Divide dough in half. Roll out on wax paper into two rectangles ¼-inch thick. Spread with cooled date-nut filling. Roll like jelly roll. Wrap in wax paper and chill overnight. Cut each roll into 45 slices. Place on greased baking sheet. Bake at 400 degrees for 10 minutes.

YIELD: 7½ DOZEN COOKIES

Coconut Cherry Bars

1¼ cups flour

½ cup butter, softened

3 tablespoons powdered sugar

2 eggs

1 cup sugar

1 teaspoon vanilla

½ teaspoon baking powder

¼ teaspoon salt

¾ cup pecans, chopped

½ cup coconut, flaked

½ cup maraschino cherries, chopped

Preheat oven to 350 degrees. Combine 1 cup flour, butter, and powdered sugar in bowl. Press mixture into greased 8-inch square baking pan. Bake for 7 to 10 minutes or until lightly browned. Cool. Beat eggs until thick and foamy. Add remaining ingredients, mixing well. Spread over baked layer. Bake for 25 minutes. Cut into bars.

Yield: 2 dozen bars

Aunt Jean's Nutties

1 cup butter

1 cup sugar

3 eggs

1 cup flour

1 teaspoon baking powder

2 cups pecans, finely ground

Zest of 1 large lemon

1 cup pecans, chopped

Preheat oven to 275 degrees. Cream butter and add sugar gradually. Set aside one egg white. Beat remaining eggs into sugar mixture. Add flour and baking powder. Blend well. Stir in ground pecans and lemon zest. Roll thin on board dusted with flour and sugar. Brush with beaten egg white. Sprinkle with chopped pecans. Cut into 1¼-inch squares. Bake on greased cookie sheet for 8 to 10 minutes or until golden brown.

Yield: 12 dozen squares

Christmas Cherryettes

¾ cup shortening

¼ cup butter

½ cup powdered sugar

1 teaspoon salt

2 tablespoons vanilla

2 cups flour

1 cup pecans, finely chopped

20 candied cherries, halved

Preheat oven to 325 degrees. In medium bowl, cream shortening and butter. Cream in powdered sugar. Add salt and vanilla. Mix well. Add flour and pecans and mix into soft dough. Shape into 1-inch balls. Place on greased baking sheet. Press hole in center of each cookie. Place candied cherry half in each. Bake for 18 minutes.

YIELD: 40 COOKIES

Orange Snowballs

2¾ cups vanilla wafers, finely crushed

1 cup powdered sugar

¼ cup butter, melted

1 cup pecans, chopped

¼ cup frozen orange juice concentrate, undiluted

3 tablespoons light corn syrup

Zest of 1 orange

1 cup powdered sugar

Combine all but final ingredient and mix well. Form into walnut-sized balls. Roll in powdered sugar. Store uncovered on counter for several hours, then store in refrigerator.

Yield: 6 dozen cookies

Pecan Angels

2 egg whites

2 cups powdered sugar, sifted

1 teaspoon vanilla

1 teaspoon vinegar

2 cups pecan halves

Preheat oven to 300 degrees. Beat egg whites until stiff. Gradually beat in powdered sugar, vanilla, and vinegar. Gently fold in pecans. Drop teaspoonfuls onto greased cookie sheet 2 inches apart. Bake for 12 to 15 minutes.

Yield: 3½ dozen cookies

Gumdrop Cookies

2 tablespoons water

4 eggs

2 cups brown sugar

2 cups flour, sifted

¼ teaspoon salt

1 cup gumdrops, chopped

¾ cup chopped pecans or walnuts

4 tablespoons butter

2 cups powdered sugar

2 tablespoons orange juice

Add water to eggs and beat until light and fluffy. Add sugar and mix well. Add sifted flour and salt. Stir in gumdrops and nuts. Pour into greased 13 x 9-inch pan. Bake for 25 minutes. Cream butter, powdered sugar, and orange juice to make icing. Spread over top while bars are still warm. Cool and cut into squares.

YIELD: 2 DOZEN BARS

Aunt Dot's Christmas Cookies

4 egg whites

1 cup flour

1 cup sugar

1 teaspoon baking powder

1 tablespoon vanilla

3 cups dates

3 cups dried cherries

3 cups dried pineapple

3 cups mixed nuts

Preheat oven to 350 degrees. Using mixer, beat egg whites until soft peaks form. Fold in remaining ingredients, mixing after each. Drop teaspoonfuls onto greased cookie sheet. Bake for 12 to 15 minutes or until light brown. Baking times vary, so check often. Cool completely. Store in airtight container.

YIELD: 8 DOZEN COOKIES

On the seventh day of Christmas my true love sent to me. . .

Seven Desserts a-Delighting

Love makes Christmas a delight!

UNKNOWN

Heavenly Father, Christmas is not only a celebration
of Your birth; it is also a celebration of love—
sacrificial, unending love. May we offer to others
Your love that has so freely been given to us. Amen.

Blessed the guest at home in your place!
We expect our fill of good things in your house.

PSALM 65:4 MSG

Festive Cherry Nut Cake

1 cup butter

2 cups sugar

4 cups flour

2 teaspoons baking powder

1 teaspoon nutmeg

1 cup orange juice

1½ cups golden raisins

2 cups pecans, shelled

1 cup maraschino cherries

Preheat oven to 325 degrees. Cream butter and sugar. Set aside 1 cup flour and combine remaining 3 cups flour with baking powder and nutmeg, mixing well. Add orange juice and mix well. Toss raisins and pecans in reserved 1 cup flour. Add to mixture and mix well. Pour into greased 13 x 9-inch baking pan. Bake on upper oven rack for two hours with a pan of water on lower oven rack. When cool, decorate with cherries.

YIELD: 12 TO 15 SERVINGS

Grandma Jan's Yam Pie

2 cups yams, cooked and mashed

1 cup sugar

2 eggs

¾ cup milk

¼ cup butter, melted

¼ teaspoon salt

1 teaspoon vanilla

1 (9 inch) unbaked pie shell

Preheat oven to 350 degrees. Combine yams, sugar, eggs, milk, butter, salt, and vanilla in blender until smooth. Pour yam mixture into pie shell. Bake for 1 hour or until set.

YIELD: 6 TO 8 SERVINGS

Aunt Linda's Christmas Cake

3 cups flour

2 cups sugar

1 teaspoon salt

1 teaspoon baking soda

1 teaspoon cinnamon

3 eggs, beaten

1½ cups vegetable oil

1 (8 ounce) can crushed pineapple, undrained

1½ teaspoons vanilla

2 cups bananas, mashed

2 cups pecans, chopped

Preheat oven to 350 degrees. Combine flour, sugar, salt, baking soda, and cinnamon in large mixing bowl. Add eggs and oil, stirring until mixture is well moistened. (Do not beat.) Stir in pineapple, vanilla, banana, and 1 cup pecans. Spoon batter into three well-greased and floured 9-inch round pans. Bake for 25 to 30 minutes. Cool in pans for 10 minutes. Remove from pans and cool completely. Spread your favorite cream cheese frosting between layers and on top and sides. Sprinkle with remaining pecans.

YIELD: 12 TO 15 SERVINGS

Chocolate Peppermint Pie

1 tablespoon unflavored gelatin

¼ cup cold water

1½ squares unsweetened chocolate, chopped

1 cup prepared coffee

2 eggs, separated

⅔ cup sugar

1 teaspoon vanilla

3 drops peppermint flavoring

¼ teaspoon salt

1 cup walnuts, finely chopped

1 (9 inch) baked pie shell

Sweetened whipped cream

Peppermint candy, crushed

Soften gelatin in cold water and combine with chocolate and coffee in small saucepan. Stir over medium heat until chocolate melts and gelatin dissolves. Remove from heat. Beat egg yolks. Beat in ⅓ cup sugar, vanilla, peppermint flavoring, and salt. Add to chocolate mixture, beating well. Set aside to cool. Beat egg whites to soft peaks. Beat in remaining ⅓ cup sugar to make meringue. When chocolate mixture is thickened, fold in meringue and ¾ cup walnuts. Pour into pie shell. Sprinkle remaining ¼ cup walnuts on top. Chill for 2 hours. Top with whipped cream and crushed peppermint.

YIELD: 6 TO 8 SERVINGS

Bûche de Noel

1 cup walnuts, finely grated

¼ cup flour

¼ cup unsweetened cocoa

5 large eggs, separated

½ teaspoon salt

¼ teaspoon cream of tartar

⅔ cup sugar, divided

½ teaspoon vanilla

2 tablespoons powdered sugar

1 cup heavy cream

¼ cup powdered sugar

½ teaspoon vanilla

¼ cup candied cherries, chopped

2 teaspoons unsweetened cocoa

2 teaspoons butter, melted

1½ teaspoons boiling water

1 tablespoon light corn syrup

¾ cup powdered sugar

Preheat oven to 350 degrees. Add walnuts to flour and coca. Beat egg whites, salt, and cream of tartar until barely stiff. Gradually beat in ⅓ cup sugar. In separate bowl, beat yolks, remaining ⅓ cup sugar, and vanilla until thick. Fold into whites. Fold in walnut mixture. Pour into 15 x 10-inch jelly roll pan lined with parchment paper. Bake for 20 minutes. Sprinkle powdered sugar on a cloth. Turn out onto cloth and roll up loosely. Refrigerate. Beat cream, powdered sugar, and vanilla until soft peaks form. Fold in cherries. Mix cocoa, butter, and boiling water. Stir in corn syrup and powdered sugar. Unroll cake. Spread with cream. Reroll. Frost with glaze.

Yield: 12 servings

Dark and Light Fruitcake

½ cup shortening

¼ cup butter

1 cup sugar

2 teaspoons vanilla

3 eggs

2 cups flour

1 teaspoon salt

1 teaspoon baking powder

2 tablespoons cooking sherry

1 cup candied pineapple, diced

1 cup whole candied cherries

1 cup pecan pieces, divided

1 cup walnut pieces, divided

2 tablespoons unsweetened cocoa

2 tablespoons boiling water

1 cup fresh dates, quartered

Preheat oven to 300 degrees. Line large loaf pan with parchment paper. Cream shortening, butter, sugar, and vanilla. Beat in eggs, one at a time. Combine flour, salt, and baking powder. Incorporate into creamed mixture alternately with sherry. Divide batter in half. Stir pineapple, cherries, ½ cup pecans, and ½ cup walnuts into first portion. Pour into prepared pan. Blend cocoa with water and stir into remaining batter. Add remaining nuts and dates. Spread in pan on top of light batter. Bake for 2 hours. Cool in pan. Store for several days before cutting.

YIELD: 12 TO 15 SERVINGS

Cindy's Christmas Bread Pudding

<hr/>

1 small orange	2 cups heavy cream
2 cups cranberries	¼ cup flour
1⅔ cups sugar	10 slices white bread
½ teaspoon almond extract	Christmas cookie cutters
3 eggs	

Preheat oven to 325 degrees. Peel and section orange. Remove pith and place orange sections and peel in food processor. Add cranberries. Process until coarsely chopped. In large bowl, combine cranberry mixture with ⅔ cup sugar and almond extract. Mix well. In separate bowl, beat together remaining 1 cup sugar, eggs, cream, and flour. Cut crusts from bread slices. Place half the bread in greased 9-inch square baking dish. Spread cranberry mixture over bread. Pour half the egg mixture over cranberry mixture. Use cookie cutters to cut remaining bread into Christmas shapes. Place on top. Pour remaining egg mixture over bread. Bake for 65 minutes.

YIELD: 12 SERVINGS

Streusel Pumpkin Pie

* * * ❄ * ❄ * * * ❄ * *

2 (9 inch) frozen deep-dish
   piecrusts, thawed

1 (16 ounce) can pumpkin

2 eggs

1 (12 ounce) can evaporated milk

¾ cup plus 2 tablespoons sugar

3 teaspoons pumpkin pie spice

¼ cup walnuts, chopped

Preheat oven to 375 degrees and place empty cookie sheet in oven. Line 1
deep-dish pie pan with crust. In large bowl, beat together pumpkin, eggs,
milk, ¾ cup sugar, and 2 teaspoons pumpkin pie spice. Pour into crust. Place
on preheated cookie sheet and bake for 30 minutes. Crumble second crust
into very small pieces. Add remaining 2 tablepsoons sugar, 1 teaspoon spice,
and walnuts. Mix well. Sprinkle over pie. Bake for another 30 to 40 minutes
or until set.

YIELD: 6 TO 8 SERVINGS

Cinnamon Baked Apples

* * * ❄ * ❄ * * * ❄ * *

4 large Granny Smith, Honey Crisp,
   or Pink Lady apples

¼ cup molasses

¼ cup sugar

2 tablespoons lemon juice

¼ teaspoon cinnamon

¼ teaspoon nutmeg

Preheat oven to 350 degrees. Core apples and remove peel on top third
of each. Place in 1½-quart baking dish. In small bowl, combine remaining
ingredients. Mix well. Pour over apples. Bake for 20 minutes. Turn apples
over. Bake 20 minutes longer. Turn right side up on serving plate. Spoon
sauce from bottom of dish over apples.

YIELD: 4 SERVINGS

Pumpkin Roll

3 eggs

1 cup sugar

⅔ cup pumpkin puree

1 teaspoon lemon juice

¾ cup flour

2 teaspoons baking powder

½ teaspoon salt

1 teaspoon ginger

1 teaspoon nutmeg

1¼ cups powdered sugar

5 teaspoons butter, softened

1 (8 ounce) package cream cheese, softened

½ teaspoon vanilla

Preheat oven to 375 degrees. Beat eggs on high speed for 5 minutes. Add sugar gradually, continuing to beat on high speed. Stir in pumpkin and lemon juice. Combine flour, baking powder, salt, and spices in separate bowl and add to pumpkin mixture. Pour into greased and floured 15 x 10-inch jelly roll pan. Bake for 15 minutes. Invert on towel sprinkled with ¼ cup powdered sugar. Roll cake and towel from short side. Cool. Cream butter and cream cheese until light and fluffy. Add remaining 1 cup powdered sugar and vanilla, mixing well. Unroll cake. Spread with creamed mixture. Roll again without towel. Place seam down on serving dish. Chill.

Yield: 10 servings

Aunt Jo's Banana Cake

½ cup shortening

1½ cups sugar

2 large bananas, cut into chunks

2 eggs

2 teaspoons vanilla

2 cups flour

½ teaspoon baking powder

¾ teaspoon baking soda

½ teaspoon salt

Preheat oven to 350 degrees. In large bowl, cream shortening and sugar. Add bananas and blend until smooth. Beat in eggs until batter is creamy. Add vanilla. In separate bowl, combine flour, baking powder, baking soda, and salt. Combine with banana mixture. Pour into greased and floured 11 x 9-inch baking pan. Bake for 30 to 35 minutes.

YIELD: 12 TO 16 SERVINGS

Curried Fruit with Almonds

* * *

1 (29 ounce) can sliced peaches, drained

2 (8 ounce) cans pineapple chunks, drained

1 (16 ounce) can pear halves, drained

1 (6 ounce) jar maraschino cherries, drained

½ cup almonds, slivered and toasted

½ cup butter, melted

¾ cup brown sugar, packed

1 tablespoon red curry powder

Preheat oven to 350 degrees. Arrange fruit in medium baking dish and sprinkle with almonds. Mix together butter, brown sugar, and curry powder. Sprinkle over fruit. Bake for 1 hour.

Yield: 8 servings

Fresh Fig Roll

* * *

1 cup fresh figs, mashed

12 large marshmallows, cut into small pieces

½ cup pecans, chopped

2 teaspoons lemon juice

1⅓ cups graham cracker crumbs

Combine figs, marshmallows, pecans, and lemon juice. Set aside ⅓ cup crumbs. Add remaining 1 cup crumbs to fig mixture and mix well. On large sheet of wax paper, sprinkle reserved crumbs. Place fig mixture on top of crumbs. Using wax paper, shape mixture into roll. Chill until firm. Slice just before serving.

Yield: 10 servings

Christmas Honey Cake

1 cup butter, softened

1 cup light brown sugar, firmly packed

6 eggs, separated

1 cup honey

1 cup sour cream

3¼ cups flour

2 teaspoons baking powder

2 teaspoons baking soda

1 teaspoon nutmeg

1 teaspoon cinnamon

¼ teaspoon salt

1 cup walnuts, chopped

1 teaspoon vanilla

1½ cups powdered sugar

2 tablespoons fresh lemon juice

Preheat oven to 350 degrees. In large bowl, cream butter until fluffy. Add brown sugar and egg yolks gradually. Stir in honey and sour cream. Beat in flour, baking powder, baking soda, spices, and salt. Fold in walnuts and vanilla. Fold in stiffly beaten egg whites. Pour into greased and floured 10 x 4-inch tube pan. Bake for 1 hour. Cool for 10 minutes before removing from pan. Combine powdered sugar and lemon juice. Spoon over top.

Yield: 12 to 15 servings

Apple Dumplings

2 cups flour

2½ teaspoons baking powder

½ teaspoon salt

½ cup shortening

¼ cup milk

8 apples, peeled and cored

8 tablespoons sugar

8 teaspoons butter

¼ cup sugar

1 teaspoon cinnamon

Preheat oven to 400 degrees. Combine flour, baking powder, and salt. Cut in shortening. Add milk and stir. Knead gently on floured board. Roll out to ⅛-inch thickness. Cut into 8 square pieces. Place one apple on each piece of dough. Fill each apple hollow with mixture of 1 tablespoon sugar and 1 teaspoon butter. Fold dough over apple. Press edges together to seal. Place in shallow baking pan. Mix together sugar and cinnamon. Sprinkle on top. Bake for 35 minutes.

YIELD: 8 SERVINGS

Granny Gin's Cranberry Pudding

1⅓ cups flour

2 cups cranberries, cut lengthwise

½ cup molasses

2 tablespoons baking soda

⅓ cup hot water

1 cup sugar

1 cup half-and-half

¼ cup butter

Sprinkle ⅓ cup flour over cranberries. Add molasses and stir. Mix baking soda with hot water and add to cranberry mixture. Stir. Add remaining 1 cup flour. Stir. Pour into double boiler and steam for 1½ hours. When pudding is almost done, combine sugar, half-and-half, and butter in small saucepan. Bring to a boil and cook for 12 minutes, stirring constantly. Pour over pudding before serving.

YIELD: 4 SERVINGS

Holiday Sauce

3 cups water

1 cup prunes

½ cup raisins

1 cup apples, chopped

1 cup pears, chopped

¼ cup sugar

1 teaspoon cinnamon

½ cup walnuts

¼ cup butter

2 tablespoons flour

In large saucepan, bring water to a boil. Add prunes and raisins. Cook for 10 minutes. Add apples, pears, sugar, cinnamon, and walnuts. Cook until fruit is tender. In small saucepan, melt butter, stir in flour, and cook until lightly brown. Add to fruit and mix well.

YIELD: 4 SERVINGS

Nut Torte

6 tablespoons flour

1 teaspoon cream of tartar

2 cups pecans or walnuts, ground

10 eggs, separated

1¼ cups sugar

1 teaspoon vanilla

Preheat oven to 350 degrees. Sift flour with cream of tartar. Mix in ground nuts. In large bowl, beat egg yolks, adding sugar gradually. (This may take 10 minutes or more.) Stir in vanilla. In another large bowl, beat egg whites until stiff. Gently stir flour mixture into yolks. Fold in egg whites. Line bottom of greased 10-inch tube pan with wax paper and pour in batter. Bake for 50 minutes. Invert pan on rack and cool.

YIELD: 12 TO 15 SERVINGS

Green Grape Cobbler

1 cup flour

½ cup sugar

2 teaspoons baking powder

¾ cup milk

1 teaspoon vanilla

2½ cups water

2 cups seedless green grapes

1½ cups sugar

¼ teaspoon salt

2 tablespoons butter

¼ cup sugar

½ teaspoon cinnamon

Preheat oven to 325 degrees. Combine flour, sugar, baking powder, milk, and vanilla in bowl. Transfer to greased 13 x 9-inch baking pan. In saucepan, bring water to a boil. Add grapes, sugar, and salt. Boil for 2 to 3 minutes or until grapes change color. Pour over batter. Batter will rise to top. Dot with butter. Mix together sugar and cinnamon. Sprinkle on top. Bake for 45 minutes.

YIELD: 15 SERVINGS

Chocolate Angel Dessert

1½ cups milk

2 eggs, beaten

½ cup sugar

¼ teaspoon salt

1 envelope unflavored gelatin

⅓ cup cold water

¾ cup semisweet chocolate chips

2 tablespoons rum flavoring

1½ cups whipping cream

1 (13 ounce) angel food cake

½ cup almonds, sliced

1 cup sweetened whipped cream

1 cup strawberries

In double boiler, cook milk, eggs, sugar, and salt for 10 to 15 minutes or until mixture coats a spoon, stirring often. Soften gelatin in water and add to custard mixture, stirring to dissolve. Remove 1 cup of custard and add to chocolate chips. Stir until chocolate is melted and set aside. When remaining custard is cool, add rum flavoring and chill until thickened. Whip cream and fold into custard. Tear cake into pieces and fold into custard. Pour into 13 x 9-inch pan. Drizzle with chocolate custard and sprinkle with almonds. Chill. Garnish with whipped cream and strawberries.

YIELD: 14 TO 16 SERVINGS

On the eighth day of Christmas my true love sent to me. . .

Eight Kids a-Cooking

It is good to be children sometimes, and never better than at Christmas, when its mighty Founder was a child Himself.

CHARLES DICKENS

Lord God, thank You for the little ones who make our lives so rich. They do so much to remind us of those things that are really important. They keep us grounded with their innocent minds and adorable giggles. They are walking, talking blessings sent directly from Your throne. Thank You for entrusting us with them. Amen.

Jesus, full of joy through the Holy Spirit, said, "I praise you, Father, Lord of heaven and earth, because you have hidden these things from the wise and learned, and revealed them to little children."

LUKE 10:21 NIV

Jodi's Gooey Buns

---

2 (7.4 ounce) cans buttermilk
   refrigerator biscuits

½ cup butter, melted

½ cup brown sugar

1 teaspoon cinnamon

½ cup nuts, chopped

Preheat oven to 375 degrees. Separate biscuit dough into pieces and roll into balls. Set aside. In round cake pan, pour melted butter. Mix together brown sugar, cinnamon, and nuts. Sprinkle over butter. Arrange biscuit dough balls in one layer in pan. Bake for 25 minutes. Turn upside down on plate while warm.

YIELD: 6 SERVINGS

Cheese Dreams

---

3 English muffins, split in half and
   buttered

6 slices cooked bacon, cut in half

6 thick tomato slices

6 cheese slices

On cookie sheet, put 6 muffin halves. Place under broiler and toast. Remove from oven. Add tomato slice, 2 bacon strips, and cheese slice to each one. Return to broiler until cheese melts.

YIELD: 6 SERVINGS

Barbecue Chicken

1 (1 gallon) ziplock storage bag

8 skinless chicken pieces

1 cup barbecue sauce

¼ cup orange juice

Preheat oven to 350 degrees. Place all ingredients in ziplock bag, seal, and turn bag over several times until chicken is well coated. Remove chicken from bag with tongs and place in greased 13 x 9-inch baking pan. Bake for 45 minutes.

Yield: 6 to 8 servings

Christmas Morning Muffins

1 egg

1 cup milk

¼ cup vegetable oil

2 cups flour

¼ cup sugar

3 teaspoons baking powder

1 teaspoon salt

Preheat oven to 400 degrees. Grease 12-cup muffin pan. In bowl, beat egg with fork. Add milk and oil. Stir. In another bowl, combine remaining ingredients and stir well. Stir into milk mixture until flour is moistened. Batter will be lumpy. Do not overmix. Fill muffin cups two-thirds full. Bake for 20 to 25 minutes.

YIELD: 12 MUFFINS

Candle Salad

6 lettuce leaves

6 pineapple slices

3 bananas, cut in half

6 maraschino cherries

6 toothpicks

Place each lettuce leaf on small plate. Lay 1 pineapple slice on top of each. Stand up banana half in middle of pineapple slice, cut end down. Attach 1 cherry to top of each banana with toothpick.

YIELD: 6 SERVINGS

Jolly Jelly Bean Cake

2 cups flour

¾ cup miniature jelly beans

1 cup sugar

1 cup butter, softened

1 (8 ounce) package cream cheese, softened

1 teaspoon vanilla

3 eggs

1½ teaspoons baking powder

¼ teaspoon salt

1 tablespoon powdered sugar

Preheat oven to 325 degrees. Grease and flour angel food cake pan. Spoon 2 tablespoons flour into measuring cup and toss jelly beans in flour. Set aside. In large bowl, beat sugar, butter, cream cheese, and vanilla until well blended. Add eggs one at a time, beating well after each. Add remaining flour, baking powder, and salt. Blend well. Spoon 1 cup of batter evenly over bottom of pan. Stir jelly beans into remaining batter. Spoon into pan. Bake for 55 minutes. Cool for 10 minutes. Remove from pan and cool completely. Sprinkle with powdered sugar.

YIELD: 8 TO 10 SERVINGS

Easy Peasy Chocolate Cake

3½ cups flour

2 cups sugar

5 tablespoons cocoa

1 teaspoon cinnamon

2 teaspoons baking soda

1 teaspoon salt

1 cup vegetable oil

2 teaspoons vinegar

2 teaspoons vanilla

2 cups water

Preheat oven to 350 degrees. In large bowl, combine flour, sugar, cocoa, cinnamon, baking soda, and salt. Mix well. Add oil, vinegar, vanilla, and water. Beat well. Pour into ungreased 13 x 9-inch baking pan. Bake for 40 minutes.

YIELD: 12 TO 15 SERVINGS

Bacon and Egg Pockets

4 pita bread rounds, sliced in half crosswise

8 slices bacon

8 eggs

2 tablespoons milk

½ teaspoon salt

¼ teaspoon pepper

1 cup cheddar cheese, shredded

In medium skillet, fry bacon until crisp. Place on paper towel to drain. Pour off grease. Whisk eggs with milk, salt, and pepper. Pour into skillet. Cook over medium heat, stirring constantly, until softly scrambled. Crumble in bacon. Warm pita halves in microwave. Place some cheese in bottom of each pocket. Add scrambled eggs with bacon.

Yield: 4 servings

Chocolate Pastry Bundles

1 sheet frozen puff pastry

1 (6 ounce) package semisweet
chocolate chips

¼ cup walnuts or pecans, chopped

¼ cup sugar (powdered or granular)

Preheat oven to 425 degrees. Roll out pastry into 12-inch square on lightly floured surface. Cut into four 6-inch squares. Place equal portion of chocolate chips and nuts in center of each square. Pull up corners of pastry squares above chocolate and twist. Bake on ungreased cookie sheet for 10 to 15 minutes. Sprinkle with sugar.

YIELD: 4 SERVINGS

Santa Sauce

8 medium apples, washed, peeled,
quartered, and cored

½ cup sugar

¼ teaspoon cinnamon

¼ teaspoon nutmeg

1 tablespoon Red Hot candies

Add water to saucepan until ½ inch deep. Add apples and bring to a boil. Boil for 5 minutes. Reduce heat and let apples simmer until tender. Stir in remaining ingredients and sprinkle with Red Hots.

YIELD: 4 SERVINGS

Night After Christmas Casserole

2 cups macaroni, cooked

2 cups turkey, cooked

2 (10.75 ounce) cans cream of
    mushroom soup

2 cups cheddar cheese, shredded

3 hard-boiled eggs, chopped

2 cups milk

In large bowl, combine all ingredients. Mix well. Refrigerate overnight. Pour into 11 x 9-inch baking dish. Bake for 1 hour.

YIELD: 10 SERVINGS

New Year's Eve Mac & Cheese

1½ cups uncooked macaroni

½ teaspoon salt

⅔ cup sour cream

2 cups cheddar cheese, shredded

⅔ cup milk

½ teaspoon paprika

Preheat oven to 325 degrees. Cook macaroni in boiling, salted water until tender. Drain and return to saucepan. Add sour cream, cheese, and milk. Mix well. Pour into medium ungreased baking dish. Sprinkle with paprika. Bake for 25 minutes.

Yield: 4 servings

Apple Dumpling Dessert

1 (12 ounce) can refrigerator biscuits

2 cups apples, peeled and thinly sliced

½ cup brown sugar, packed

½ cup evaporated milk

½ cup dark corn syrup

¼ cup butter

Whipped cream

Preheat oven to 375 degrees. Separate biscuits and place in greased 8-inch square baking pan. Arrange apple slices on top of biscuits. In small saucepan, combine brown sugar, milk, corn syrup, and butter. Bring to a boil. Pour over apples. Bake for 30 minutes. Serve warm, topped with whipped cream.

Yield: 10 servings

Berry Smoothie

2 cups milk

⅔ cup berries (any kind)

2 tablespoons frozen apple juice concentrate

1 cup ice cubes

Combine all ingredients in blender and blend on medium speed until smooth.

Yield: 2 servings

PB&J Sandwich Cookies

¼ cup butter

¼ cup peanut butter

½ cup brown sugar, packed

⅓ cup honey

1 egg

½ teaspoon vanilla

1¾ cups flour

1 teaspoon baking soda

¼ teaspoon salt

½ cup strawberry or red raspberry jam

½ cup coconut, flaked

In large bowl, cream butter, peanut butter, brown sugar, and honey. Beat in egg and vanilla. In another bowl, combine flour, baking soda, and salt. Blend flour mixture into creamed mixture. Chill for 30 minutes. Preheat oven to 350 degrees. Shape dough into small balls. Place on greased baking sheet. Bake for 8 minutes. Cool completely. Put jam between 2 cookies and squeeze slightly. Roll edges in coconut.

YIELD: 2 DOZEN COOKIES

Christmas Marshmallows

2 cups sugar

3 envelopes unflavored gelatin

¼ teaspoon salt

1 cup water

1 tablespoon butter

1 teaspoon vanilla

⅓ cup powdered sugar, sifted

Red and green colored sugar

Coat 13 x 9-inch baking pan with butter. Set aside. In medium saucepan, combine sugar, gelatin, salt, and water. Mix well. Cook over medium heat, stirring often until mixture boils. Pour into large bowl and let stand for 30 minutes. Using electric mixer, beat sugar mixture for 10 minutes. Mixture should be tripled in volume and bright white. Beat in vanilla. Spoon into prepared pan. Smooth top. Cover and refrigerate for 2 hours. Use cookie cutters to create holiday shapes. Sprinkle with powdered sugar and red and green colored sugar.

YIELD: 9 SERVINGS

On the ninth day of Christmas my true love sent to me. . .

Nine Main Dishes a-Mixing

Christmas is the season for kindling
the fire of hospitality in the hall,
the genial flame of charity in the heart.

WASHINGTON IRVING

Heavenly Father, especially at Christmas we realize how much we need You in our lives, how much we count on You to meet our deepest needs, comfort our restless hearts, and shine Your light on the path before us. Thank You for helping us shoulder all the responsibilities in our lives and showing us how to be a blessing to others. Amen.

God can pour on the blessings in astonishing ways so that you're ready for anything and everything, more than just ready to do what needs to be done.

2 CORINTHIANS 9:8 MSG

Candied Ham

1 (5 to 6 pound rump or shank portion) ham

2 teaspoons orange zest

1 cup orange juice

½ cup brown sugar, packed

4 teaspoons cornstarch

1½ teaspoons dry mustard

Preheat oven to 325 degrees. Score ham by making diagonal cuts in a diamond pattern. Place ham on rack in shallow roasting pan. If using rump, bake for 1½ hours. If using shank, bake for 2 hours. In saucepan, combine remaining ingredients. Cook and stir over medium heat until thick and bubbly. Cook and stir for 2 minutes longer. Brush over ham. Bake for another 25 minutes. Internal temperature should be 135 degrees. Let stand for at least 15 minutes before carving.

YIELD: 20 SERVINGS

Festive Roast Chicken

1 (3.5 to 4 pound) whole chicken

¼ teaspoon salt

1 small onion, quartered

2 celery stalks, diced

3 tablespoons coconut oil

Dried thyme or oregano

Rinse chicken and pat dry. Rub salt inside body cavity. Fill cavity with onions and celery. Tie legs to tail. Place chicken breast side up in shallow roasting pan. Brush with oil and sprinkle with herb. Roast uncovered for 1½ hours. Remove from oven. Cover and let stand for 10 minutes before carving.

YIELD: 6 TO 8 SERVINGS

Cornish Game Hens

6 Cornish game hens, thawed

2 teaspoons salt

2 teaspoons dried rosemary

1 cup dried apricot halves

1 cup applesauce

1 cup white wine

¼ cup brown sugar, firmly packed

1 teaspoon orange zest

¼ teaspoon ground cloves

Preheat oven to 350 degrees. Wash hens under cold water. Pat dry inside and out. Sprinkle with salt and rosemary inside and out. Secure legs. Bake for 1 hour. While roasting, chop apricots. Add to applesauce and wine in a medium saucepan. Stir in brown sugar, orange zest, and cloves. Cover and simmer for about 30 minutes or until apricots are tender. Put mixture through sieve. Spoon over hens. Roast for an additional 30 minutes.

Yield: 6 servings

Teriyaki Duck

2 (2 to 3 pound) Mallard ducks, cleaned

2 tablespoons oil

3 tablespoons soy sauce

3 tablespoons teriyaki sauce

2 tablespoons honey

1 tablespoon lemon juice

¼ teaspoon ground ginger

¼ teaspoon pepper

2 garlic cloves, sliced

Place ducks in large bowl and rub with oil. In measuring cup, combine remaining ingredients. Pour over ducks. Marinate in refrigerator overnight. Remove from marinade and place on rack in roasting pan. Preheat oven to 400 degrees. Roast for 55 minutes, turning once and basting occasionally.

Yield: 4 to 6 servings

Holiday Crab Cakes

1 egg, beaten

1 egg white, beaten

1 cup soft bread crumbs

2 tablespoons mayonnaise

2 teaspoons dry dill weed

2 teaspoons spicy mustard

2 tablespoons diced green onion

1 teaspoon seafood seasoning

¼ teaspoon pepper

1 (12 ounce) container fresh lump crabmeat

Preheat oven to 450 degrees. In bowl, combine all ingredients except crabmeat. Mix well. Stir in crabmeat and shape into 5 patties. Place in greased baking dish. Bake uncovered for 10 minutes, turning over once.

Yield: 5 patties

Papa's Prawns

⅓ cup butter

4 tablespoons garlic, minced

6 green onions, thinly sliced

¼ cup white wine

2 tablespoons lemon juice

8 large parsley sprigs, chopped

16 large prawns, peeled

¼ teaspoon salt

¼ teaspoon pepper

In large skillet, combine all ingredients except prawns, salt, and pepper. Sauté on medium heat just long enough to soften garlic and onions. Add prawns. Mix well. Cook only until prawns turn pink and begin to firm up. Sprinkle with salt and pepper and remove from heat.

Yield: 4 servings

Seafood Shells

16 ounces uncooked jumbo pasta shells

½ teaspoon salt

1 (7.5 ounce) can crabmeat, drained and flaked

1 (2.5 ounce) can tiny shrimp, drained

1 cup Swiss cheese, shredded

2 tablespoons celery, chopped

½ cup mayonnaise

2 tablespoons onion, finely chopped

Boil pasta in 6 quarts of salted water until tender but firm. Drain. Rinse with cold water, drain, and invert on paper towel to dry. In bowl, combine crabmeat, shrimp, cheese, celery, mayonnaise, and onion. Mix well. Spoon mixture into each shell and place in plastic container. Cover and refrigerate until time to serve.

YIELD: 6 SERVINGS

Pork Loin with Cherry Sauce

1 (4 to 5 pound) boneless pork loin roast

½ teaspoon salt

½ teaspoon pepper

⅛ teaspoon dried thyme

1 cup cherry preserves

¼ cup red wine vinegar

2 tablespoons light corn syrup

¼ teaspoon cinnamon

¼ teaspoon nutmeg

¼ teaspoon cloves

¼ teaspoon salt

¼ cup almonds, slivered and toasted

Preheat oven to 325 degrees. Rub roast with mixture of salt, pepper, and thyme. Place on rack in 13 x 9-inch baking pan. Cook uncovered for 2½ hours. In small saucepan, combine preserves, vinegar, corn syrup, spices, and salt. Bring to a boil, stirring occasionally. Reduce heat and simmer for 2 minutes. Add almonds. Spoon sauce over roast and cook for an additional 30 minutes, basting with sauce several times.

YIELD: 10 TO 12 SERVINGS

Ham and Asparagus Rolls

6 deli ham slices, thin enough to roll but thick enough to resist tearing

24 large asparagus spears, cooked

¼ cup plus 2 tablespoons butter, melted

⅓ cup flour

1 teaspoon salt

2 teaspoons onion, minced

2 cups milk

½ cup cheddar cheese, shredded

Preheat oven to 350 degrees. Lay out ham slices on cutting board. Place 4 asparagus spears on each slice. Brush with 2 tablespoons melted butter and roll up. Place in shallow baking pan. In saucepan, combine remaining ¼ cup melted butter, flour, and salt. Blend together. Stir in onion and milk gradually. Cook on medium heat until thick, stirring constantly. Add cheese and mix well. Pour over ham rolls. Bake for 25 minutes.

YIELD: 6 SERVINGS

Fruited Pot Roast

2 tablespoons coconut oil

1 (3 to 4 pound) beef pot roast

½ cup onion, finely chopped

⅓ cup carrot, finely chopped

¼ cup red wine

1 teaspoon garlic, minced

1½ teaspoons salt

¼ teaspoon pepper

1½ cups hot water

1¾ cups mixed dried fruit

Heat oil in Dutch oven. Add roast and brown on both sides. Add onion, carrot, wine, garlic, salt, and pepper. Cover and simmer on stovetop for 2 hours. Pour hot water over dried fruit. Let stand for 1 hour. Drain. Place fruit on top of meat. Cover and cook for 1 hour longer.

YIELD: 6 SERVINGS

Herb-Rubbed Lamb Chops

1 teaspoon thyme

1 teaspoon oregano

1 teaspoon rosemary

3 small bay leaves, crushed

Zest and juice of 1 lemon

⅓ teaspoon paprika

4 loin or 8 rib lamb chops, trimmed

6 tablespoons coconut oil

¼ teaspoon salt

¼ teaspoon pepper

Mix herbs, zest, and paprika. Rub mixture into both sides of chops. Arrange in shallow dish. Combine lemon juice and oil and pour over chops. Sprinkle with salt and pepper. Marinate in refrigerator for 3 hours. Drain chops and place on grill or in broiler pan. Cook on grill or under broiler for 8 to 10 minutes on each side.

Yield: 4 servings

Garlic-Basted Roast Turkey

1 (10 to 12 pound) turkey
¼ teaspoon salt
¼ teaspoon pepper

3 tablespoons garlic, minced
½ cup butter, melted

Preheat oven to 325 degrees. Rinse turkey and pat dry. Rub salt and pepper into cavities. Tie up drumsticks. Roast 3½ hours for 10 pounds and 4 hours for 12 pounds. Mix garlic with melted butter. Baste with garlic butter every hour. Allow turkey to rest for 20 minutes before carving.

Yield: 10 to 12 servings

Holiday Ham Roll-Ups

1 cup Swiss cheese, shredded

5 cups cabbage, cooked, drained, and chopped

8 large, thin ham slices

¼ cup onion, minced

3 tablespoons butter

3 tablespoons flour

1½ cups milk

2 teaspoons brown mustard

1 tablespoon parsley, chopped

¼ cup bread crumbs

Preheat oven to 375 degrees. Combine ½ cup cheese with cabbage and spoon 3 tablespoons of mixture onto each ham slice. Roll up. Place in greased baking dish, seam side down. Sauté onions in 2 tablespoons butter. Blend in flour, milk, and mustard. Boil gently for 2 minutes, stirring constantly. Add remaining ½ cup cheese and parsley. Pour over ham rolls. Melt remaining 1 tablespoon butter and combine with bread crumbs. Sprinkle over cheese mixture and bake for 25 minutes.

YIELD: 8 ROLL-UPS

Jumbo Shrimp with Crab Stuffing

24 jumbo shrimp

1 pound crabmeat

2 green onions

⅓ cup celery leaf, chopped

Juice of ½ lemon

4 ounces cheddar cheese, cubed

1 egg

Preheat oven to 350 degrees. Clean and shell shrimp. Cut lengthwise along top. Open and flatten. Arrange in greased baking dish, cut side up. Chop remaining ingredients in food processor. Spoon on top of shrimp in mounds. Bake for 15 minutes.

YIELD: 6 SERVINGS

Chicken Breasts Cordon Bleu

2 large chicken breasts, skinned and
   deboned

⅛ teaspoon salt

⅛ teaspoon pepper

4 ham slices

4 Swiss cheese slices

1 egg

3 tablespoons water

½ cup bread crumbs

½ cup flour

½ cup Parmesan cheese

1 stick butter

⅓ cup oil

Pound chicken until flat. Sprinkle with salt and pepper. Layer ham slice and Swiss cheese slice on each. Roll up and secure with toothpick. Mix egg and water. In separate bowl combine dry ingredients and Parmesan cheese. Dip chicken in egg mixture and then dredge in flour mixture. Combine oil and butter in skillet. Fry until golden brown and cheese is melted.

Yield: 4 servings

Chicken á la Orange

8 boneless chicken breasts

⅓ cup flour

1½ teaspoons salt

1 teaspoon garlic powder

½ teaspoon paprika

⅓ cup almonds, sliced

5 tablespoons butter

1 (6 ounce) can frozen orange juice concentrate

1½ cups water

1 teaspoon dried rosemary

¼ teaspoon dried thyme

2 tablespoons cornstarch

Preheat oven to 350 degrees. Combine flour, 1 teaspoon salt, garlic powder, and paprika. Coat chicken in mixture. In large skillet, sauté almonds in butter until golden. Remove from pan. Brown chicken in drippings in same pan and place in single layer in 13 x 9-inch baking pan. Pour drippings from pan over chicken. Stir orange juice concentrate, water, rosemary, thyme, and remaining ½ teaspoon salt into pan. Heat to boiling. Pour over chicken. Cover. Bake for 1 hour. Remove from pan. Reheat liquid in pan to boiling. Thicken with cornstarch.

Yield: 8 servings

Turkey Puffs

2 tablespoons butter

2 tablespoons flour

2 cups chicken broth

¾ cup milk

2 eggs, lightly beaten

1 tablespoon Parmesan cheese, grated

3 ounces cream cheese

¼ teaspoon pepper

¼ teaspoon nutmeg

2 cups turkey, cooked and cubed

½ cup butter, melted

2 cans flaky refrigerator biscuits

Preheat oven to 375 degrees. In saucepan, melt butter and add flour gradually. Stir in broth and milk. Cook over medium heat until thickened, stirring constantly. Remove from heat. Place eggs in a bowl. Add broth mixture and stir. Return mixture to saucepan. Add cheese, pepper, nutmeg, and turkey. Brush 12-cup muffin pan with melted butter. Roll out each biscuit into 5-inch circle. Place one biscuit in each muffin cup. Spoon in turkey mixture. Fold edges of biscuits and pinch together. Brush with melted butter. Bake for 30 minutes. Cool for 5 minutes before removing.

YIELD: 12 SERVINGS

Turkey Tetrazzini

1 (8 ounce) package thin spaghetti

¼ cup onion, chopped

2 tablespoons butter

2 tablespoons flour

1 chicken bouillon cube

1 teaspoon salt

1 teaspoon dry mustard

½ teaspoon pepper

1 (12 ounce) can evaporated milk

1½ cups water

3 to 4 ounces mushrooms, sliced

3 cups turkey, cooked and diced

1 cup sharp cheddar cheese, shredded

¼ cup grated Parmesan cheese

Preheat oven to 450 degrees. Cook spaghetti and drain. Place in buttered 13 x 9-inch baking dish. Sauté onion in butter until soft. Remove from heat and blend in flour, bouillon cube, salt, mustard, and pepper. Slowly stir in evaporated milk and water. Cook, stirring constantly, until sauce thickens and boils for 1 minute. Stir in mushrooms. Pour 2 cups of sauce over spaghetti and combine remainder with turkey. Spoon over spaghetti. Sprinkle cheese on top. Bake for 20 minutes.

Yield: 6 servings

Noel Shrimp Casserole

½ pound fresh mushrooms, sliced

4 tablespoons butter

2 cups cooked shrimp

2 cups rice

1 cup green pepper, chopped

1 cup onion, chopped

½ cup celery, chopped

1 (20 ounce) can diced, stewed tomatoes, drained

¾ teaspoon salt

½ teaspoon chili powder

½ cup butter, melted

Preheat oven to 350 degrees. In large skillet, sauté mushrooms in butter until tender. Mix in shrimp, rice, vegetables, and seasonings. Pour into greased 2-quart casserole. Pour butter over top. Bake for 50 minutes.

Yield: 6 servings

Aunt Nan's Chicken Divan

6 boneless, skinless chicken breasts, cooked and cut into chunks

2 cups broccoli, blanched and drained

1 cup mayonnaise

¼ teaspoon curry powder

1 (26 ounce) can cream of chicken soup

1 cup cheddar cheese, shredded

½ teaspoon salt

1 teaspoon lemon juice

1 cup bread crumbs

2 tablespoons butter, melted

Preheat oven to 350 degrees. In 13 x 9-inch baking dish, distribute chicken and broccoli evenly. In saucepan, combine mayonnaise, curry powder, chicken soup, cheese, salt, and lemon juice. Heat until cheese is melted and mixture is smooth. Pour over chicken and broccoli. Sprinkle with bread crumbs. Pour melted butter over crumbs. Bake for 30 minutes.

YIELD: 8 SERVINGS

Shrimp Newberg

¼ cup flour

¼ cup butter

4 cups half-and-half

3 egg yolks

½ cup cooking sherry

1 pound cooked shrimp

Heat flour and butter in large saucepan. Add 2 cups half-and-half. Beat egg yolks with remaining half-and-half and gradually add to mixture. Stir constantly until sauce is slightly thickened. Add cooking sherry and shrimp.

YIELD: 4 SERVINGS

On the tenth day of Christmas my true love sent to me. . .

Ten Salads a-Crunching

Christmas is the one season of the year when
we can lay aside all gnawing worry, indulge in
sentiment without censure, assume the carefree
faith of childhood, and just plain "have fun."

D. D. MONROE

Father, help us forget ourselves this Christmas, putting aside all our petty grudges, unrealistic expectations, and prideful thoughts. Give us the grace to act like children, delighted to be in Your presence, calmed by Your peace, and amazed by all the gifts of grace You have given us. Amen.

*Grace and peace to you from God
our Father and the Lord Jesus Christ.*

1 Corinthians 1:3 niv

Frosted Fruit Salad

1 (14 ounce) can sweetened condensed milk

1 (21 ounce) can peach or cherry pie filling

1 (15 ounce) can mandarin oranges, drained

1 (20 ounce) can crushed pineapple, drained

⅔ cup pecans or walnuts, chopped

1 (8 ounce) carton frozen whipped topping, thawed

In large bowl, combine milk and pie filling, Add oranges, pineapple, and nuts. Gently fold in whipped topping. Spread in 13 x 9-inch baking dish. Cover and freeze. Remove from freezer for 15 minutes before serving. Cut into squares.

YIELD: 12 TO 15 SERVINGS

Seven Cup Salad

1 cup pineapple chunks, drained

1 cup fruit cocktail, drained

1 cup flaked coconut

1 cup mini marshmallows

1 cup cottage cheese

1 cup chopped pecans

1 cup sour cream

Combine all ingredients except sour cream. Chill for 2 hours but do not freeze. Add sour cream and stir well about 1 hour before serving.

YIELD: 7 CUPS

Aunt Sally's Jeweled Salad

1 (6 ounce) package strawberry gelatin

½ teaspoon salt

2 cups hot water

1 (8 ounce) can crushed pineapple

2 tablespoons lemon juice

Cold water

½ cup pecans, chopped

½ cup celery, diced

⅔ cup raw cranberries, chopped

Dissolve gelatin and salt in hot water. Drain pineapple, saving syrup. Combine syrup and lemon juice with cold water to make 1⅔ cups liquid. Add to gelatin. Chill until slightly thickened. Fold in pecans, celery, cranberries, and pineapple. Pour into greased mold and chill for at least 4 hours.

YIELD: 8 TO 10 SERVINGS

Minty Melon Salad

½ small watermelon

1 small honeydew melon

1 small cantaloupe

2 cups grapefruit juice

3 tablespoons honey

Mint sprigs

Using melon baller, remove melon meat and mix in large serving bowl. In small saucepan, combine juice with enough honey to sweeten as desired. Heat just until honey is dissolved. Cool and pour over melons. Chill. Garnish with mint sprigs.

Yield: 8 to 12 servings

Lemon-Lime Melon Salad

2 teaspoons lime zest

6 tablespoons lime juice

¼ cup frozen orange juice
concentrate

½ teaspoon vanilla

1 cantaloupe

1 honeydew melon

2 cups seedless grapes

Combine lime zest, lime juice, orange juice, and vanilla in large bowl. Set aside. Cut melons in half. Slice each half into 1-inch wedges. Remove rind. Cut into ¾-inch pieces. Add grapes. Pour lime mixture over melon pieces and toss. Chill until ready to serve.

YIELD: 8 SERVINGS

Snowed-In Salad

1 small head cauliflower, broken
into pieces

1 medium onion, sliced

2 white radishes, sliced

1 small cucumber, sliced

1 cup sour cream

2 teaspoons lemon juice

2 tablespoons sugar

½ teaspoon salt

¼ teaspoon white pepper

Combine first four ingredients in bowl. In separate bowl, combine sour cream with remaining ingredients. Mix well. Let stand for 1 hour. Pour over salad.

YIELD: 6 SERVINGS

Cucumber Yogurt Salad

1½ teaspoons salt

3 cucumbers, unpeeled and thinly sliced

2 tablespoons parsley, chopped

¾ teaspoon dill weed

½ teaspoon garlic salt

½ cup plain yogurt

Sprinkle salt over cucumbers. Toss. Chill for 30 minutes, tossing occasionally. Combine chopped parsley, dill weed, garlic salt, and yogurt. Drain cucumber well. Stir in yogurt dressing. Garnish with additional parsley if desired.

YIELD: 4 TO 6 SERVINGS

Gazpacho Salad

2 large tomatoes, peeled and coarsely chopped

1 small cucumber, peeled and coarsely chopped

½ medium onion, finely chopped

½ green pepper, chopped

1 cup tomato juice

1 tablespoon wine vinegar

½ teaspoon salt

⅛ teaspoon pepper

Combine all ingredients in large bowl. Cover and refrigerate to blend flavors before serving. Will keep for 2 to 3 days in refrigerator.

Yield: 4 servings

Sally's Strawberry Salad

2 (10 ounce) packages frozen strawberries

2 (8 ounce) cans crushed pineapple

1 (6 ounce) package strawberry gelatin

½ cup sugar

1 cup mini marshmallows

3 bananas, sliced

½ cup pecans, chopped

1 (16 ounce) carton sour cream

1 (8 ounce) package cream cheese, softened

Drain strawberries and pineapple, reserving juice. Add enough water to juice to measure 2 cups. In saucepan, bring juice mixture to a boil. Dissolve gelatin, sugar, and marshmallows in juice mixture. Chill in pan until partially set. Fold in fruit and pecans. In decorative serving bowl, pour small amount of fruit mixture. Chill until firm. Blend sour cream and cream cheese. Pour half on top of fruit mixture. Add remaining fruit mixture. Chill until firm. Top with remaining cream mixture.

YIELD: 12 SERVINGS

Peach Ambrosia

8 medium fresh peaches or 2 (16 ounce) cans sliced peaches

1 cup bananas, sliced

2 tablespoons sugar

2 tablespoons lemon juice

⅓ cup coconut, flaked

Peel and slice peaches. Combine peaches, bananas, sugar, and lemon juice. Chill. Spoon into serving dish and top with flaked coconut.

YIELD: 6 TO 8 SERVINGS

Cranberry Fruit Relish

2 cups fresh cranberries

1 medium apple, peeled and
    chopped

⅓ cup raisins

¼ cup orange juice

1 tablespoon sugar

1 (8 ounce) can crushed pineapple,
    drained

1 medium orange, sectioned

Combine cranberries, apple, raisins, orange juice, and sugar in saucepan. Simmer for 20 minutes. Remove from heat. Stir in pineapple and orange. Cover and chill for 48 hours.

YIELD: 6 SERVINGS

Christmas Cranberry Salad

1 (14 ounce) can sweetened
  condensed milk

¼ cup lemon juice

1 (20 ounce) can crushed pineapple,
  drained

1 (16 ounce) can whole-berry
  cranberry sauce

2 cups mini marshmallows

½ cup chopped pecans

Red food coloring, optional

1 (8 ounce) carton frozen whipped
  topping, thawed

Combine milk and lemon juice in bowl. Mix well. Add pineapple, cranberry sauce, marshmallows, pecans, and food coloring. Stir well. Fold in whipped topping. Transfer to 13 x 9-inch baking dish. Freeze for 4 hours. Cut into squares.

Yield: 12 to 16 servings

Cool Christmas Delight

1 (8 ounce) container small-curd
cottage cheese

1 (3 ounce) package strawberry
gelatin

1 (8 ounce) container frozen
whipped topping, thawed

1 (8 ounce) can crushed pineapple

1 (8 ounce) package frozen
strawberries, thawed and drained

1 cup pecans, chopped

Mix cottage cheese and gelatin together in large bowl. Add whipped topping
and mix well. Add pineapple, strawberries, and pecans and mix well. Chill
until ready to scrve.

Yield: 6 servings

Crunchy Pear Salad

6 pears

2 tablespoons lemon juice

1 cup celery, chopped

½ cup walnuts, chopped

¼ cup olives, chopped

½ cup mayonnaise

Salad greens

Core pears and trim tops. Sprinkle 1 teaspoon lemon juice over each.
Combine celery, walnuts, olives, and mayonnaise. Fill each pear with celery
mixture. Serve on greens.

Yield: 6 servings

Bean Salad

1⅓ cups fine cracker crumbs

1 (16 ounce) can kidney beans, drained

⅓ cup sweet pickle, chopped

¼ cup green onion, sliced

1 cup cheddar cheese, shredded

½ cup mayonnaise

Preheat oven to 450 degrees. Set aside ⅓ cup cracker crumbs. Combine remaining 1 cup crumbs, beans, pickle, onion, cheese, and mayonnaise. Toss lightly and spoon into greased 1-quart baking dish. Sprinkle with reserved crumbs. Bake for 10 minutes.

YIELD: 4 SERVINGS

Apple Coconut Salad

3 apples, chopped

1 cup celery, diced

½ cup coconut, flaked

1 tablespoon lemon juice

1 tablespoon sugar

¼ cup coconut oil

¼ cup orange juice

¼ teaspoon salt

¼ teaspoon paprika

Combine apples, celery, and coconut. Combine lemon juice and sugar in separate bowl and sprinkle over fruit. Combine oil, orange juice, salt, and paprika. Add to fruit and mix well. Chill.

YIELD: 6 SERVINGS

Festive Rice Salad

3 cups cooked long grain rice

1 (20 ounce) bag frozen peas, cooked and drained

1 (6 ounce) bag frozen cooked tiny shrimp, thawed

1 cup mayonnaise

¾ cup celery, diced

2 tablespoons chopped onion

⅛ teaspoon salt

⅛ teaspoon pepper

Lettuce

Lightly mix together rice, peas, shrimp, mayonnaise, celery, and onion. Season to taste with salt and pepper. Chill and serve over lettuce of your choice.

YIELD: 4 SERVINGS

Holiday Fruit Medley

½ cup French dressing

2 tablespoons light brown sugar

¼ teaspoon cinnamon

½ cup fresh pineapple chunks

1 peach, cut into slices

2 kiwi, peeled and sliced

1 cup cantaloupe chunks

½ cup strawberry halves

8 thin pineapple slices, peeled

8 thin cantaloupe slices, peeled

Stir together dressing, brown sugar, and cinnamon until smooth. Toss pineapple chunks, peach, kiwi, cantaloupe chunks, and strawberries with dressing. Arrange remaining fruit on serving dish. Top with marinated fruit mixture.

Yield: 6 servings

Carbonated Fruit Salad

---

1 envelope unflavored gelatin

2 tablespoons sugar

¼ cup water

Juice of 1 lemon

1½ cups cola or ginger ale

1½ cups mixed fruit, diced

In saucepan, combine gelatin and sugar. Add water and lemon juice. Stirring constantly, place over low heat until sugar and gelatin dissolve. Remove from heat. Add cola or ginger ale. Chill until slightly thickened. Fold in mixed diced fruit and chill until firm.

YIELD: 6 SERVINGS

Frosted Grapes

1 bunch extra-large seedless red or green grapes

1 egg white

1 cup sugar

Pull grapes from bunch or process them in small bunches. Rinse thoroughly and pat dry. Beat egg white until frothy. Dip grapes in egg white and shake off excess. Then dip in sugar.

Orange Apricot Salad

2 (3 ounce) packages orange gelatin

2 cups hot water

½ cup peach or apricot juice

½ cup pineapple juice

1 (15 ounce) can apricots, drained and finely chopped

1 (8 ounce) can crushed pineapple

½ cup apricot juice

½ cup pineapple juice

2 tablespoons flour

1 egg

2 tablespoons butter

½ cup sugar

2 cups cream, whipped until soft peaks form

In bowl, dissolve gelatin in hot water. Add peach (or apricot) and pineapple juice. Pour into 11 x 7-inch glass baking dish. Let set in refrigerator. Add apricots and pineapple. In saucepan, combine apricot juice, pineapple juice, flour, egg, butter, and sugar. Cook until sugar is dissolved and egg has been incorporated and cooked. Cool. Fold in 2 cups of whipped cream. Spread reamining whipeed cream over gelatin. Chill.

Yield: 15 servings

On the eleventh day of Christmas my true love sent to me. . .

It isn't the holly, it isn't the snow.
It isn't the tree nor the firelight's glow.
It's the warmth that comes to the hearts of men
when the Christmas spirit returns again.

UNKNOWN

Dear Jesus, help us this Christmas as we strive to remain free of all the negatives that accompany the season—stress, selfishness, pride, envy, busyness—and focus on our love for You. Help us celebrate Your generous heart by reaching out to bless others as You have so richly blessed us. Amen.

[Jesus] said, "That you love the Lord your God with all your passion and prayer and muscle and intelligence— and that you love your neighbor as well as you do yourself."

LUKE 10:27 MSG

Green Beans with Walnuts

1 pound green beans, cooked and salted

1 (10 ounce) can cream of mushroom soup

⅓ cup walnuts, chopped

1 cup soft bread crumbs

1 tablespoon butter, melted

Preheat oven to 375 degrees. Mix beans with soup and walnuts. Pour into greased casserole dish. Sprinkle crumbs on top. Drizzle butter over crumbs. Bake for 20 to 25 minutes.

YIELD: 4 SERVINGS

Wild Rice Casserole

¼ cup green onions (whites only)

1 cup celery, chopped

2 tablespoons butter

1 cup uncooked wild rice

2 (10 ounce) cans cream of mushroom soup

1 (4 ounce) can sliced mushrooms, drained

1½ cups Swiss cheese, shredded

3 tablespoons cooking sherry

¾ cup pecans, chopped

Preheat oven to 325 degrees. Sauté onions and celery in butter. Add rice, soup, mushrooms, cheese, sherry, and pecans. Mix well and pour into greased 3-quart casserole dish. Cover and bake for 1 hour and 15 minutes.

YIELD: 6 TO 8 SERVINGS

Blue Cheese Deviled Eggs

8 hard-boiled eggs

⅓ cup blue cheese, crumbled

⅓ cup sour cream

¾ teaspoon cider vinegar

Lettuce cups

Peel eggs and cut lengthwise. Remove yolks and set aside whites. Mash yolks and cheese. Blend in sour cream and vinegar. Fill each half egg white with yolk mixture. Cover and chill. Serve in lettuce cups.

Yield: 4 servings

Cheddar Carrots

2 cups carrots, cooked and mashed

1 cup cracker crumbs

1 cup milk

¾ cup sharp cheddar cheese, shredded

1 cup butter, softened

¼ cup onion, grated

1 teaspoon salt

⅛ teaspoon cayenne pepper

¼ teaspoon ground black pepper

3 eggs

Preheat oven to 350 degrees. Combine carrots, crumbs, milk, cheese, butter, onion, salt, and peppers and mix well. Beat eggs until thick. Fold into carrot mixture. Pour into greased 8-inch baking dish. Bake for 40 minutes.

YIELD: 8 SERVINGS

Christmas Yams

½ cup flour

½ cup brown sugar, packed

½ cup quick oats

1 teaspoon cinnamon

⅓ cup butter

2 (17 ounce) cans yams, drained

2 cups fresh cranberries

1½ cups mini marshmallows

Preheat oven to 350 degrees. Combine flour, brown sugar, oats, and cinnamon in bowl. Cut in butter. In separate bowl combine yams and cranberries. Stir in 1 cup of flour mixture. Pour into 8-inch or 9-inch baking dish. Sprinkle with remaining flour mixture. Bake for 35 minutes. Sprinkle marshmallows evenly on top. Place under broiler until lightly browned.

Yield: 8 servings

Hajovsky Holiday Potatoes

2 pounds frozen hash browns, thawed

½ cup butter, melted

1 teaspoon salt

½ teaspoon pepper

¼ cup onion, chopped

1 (10.75 ounce) can cream of chicken soup

¾ cup milk

1 cup sour cream

1 cup cheddar cheese, shredded

Preheat oven to 350 degrees. In large bowl, combine all ingredients and mix well. Pour into 14 x 9-inch baking dish. Bake for 20 minutes.

Yield: 8 servings

Golden Potatoes

5 medium potatoes, peeled, boiled, and sliced

2 tablespoons butter

2 red onions, chopped

2 tablespoons flour

½ teaspoon salt

½ teaspoon pepper

1 cup half-and-half

1 tablespoon Dijon mustard

½ cup mayonnaise

4 slices bacon, cooked and crumbled

1 teaspoon dried thyme

Preheat oven to 350 degrees. Place boiled potatoes in buttered 1½-quart baking dish. Set aside. In saucepan, melt butter and sauté onions until soft. Sprinkle with flour. Stir in salt and pepper. Add half-and-half slowly, stirring constantly until thickened. Remove from heat and cool slightly. Add mustard and mayonnaise, blending well. Pour over potatoes. Bake for 30 minutes. Sprinkle with bacon and thyme.

Yield: 8 servings

Baked Asparagus

1 pound fresh asparagus, chopped

½ teaspoon salt

1 teaspoon white pepper

2 eggs, beaten

1 cup buttery cracker crumbs

1 cup milk

1 cup cheddar cheese, shredded

¼ cup butter, melted

Preheat oven to 400 degrees. Boil asparagus in water until almost tender. Drain. Add remaining ingredients and mix well. Spoon into greased 8-inch square baking dish. Bake for 30 minutes.

Yield: 6 servings

Marshmallow Sweet Potatoes

4 cups sweet potatoes, cooked and
  mashed

½ cup butter

¼ cup evaporated milk

½ cup sugar

¾ cup pecans

1 teaspoon cinnamon

2 cups mini marshmallows

Preheat oven to 350 degrees. Combine all ingredients except marshmallows and mix well. Pour into greased casserole dish and top with marshmallows. Bake just until marshmallows are browned.

YIELD: 8 SERVINGS

Fancy Butternut Squash

1 large butternut squash

⅓ cup light brown sugar, packed

¼ cup butter

1 cup crushed pineapple

½ teaspoon salt

Peel squash and cut in half. Remove seeds and cut into cubes. Place in large saucepan and cover with water. Bring to a boil, cover pan, and lower heat. Cook for 45 minutes. Drain and puree cooked squash in food processor. Pour back into saucepan. Stir in brown sugar, butter, pineapple, and salt. Cook over low heat until hot.

YIELD: 6 SERVINGS

Creamed Onions and Peas

24 small boiler onions, peeled

1½ cups chicken broth

¼ cup butter, softened

6 tablespoons flour

1 cup sour cream

1 (10 ounce) package frozen peas

¼ teaspoon salt

¼ teaspoon pepper

In saucepan, combine onions and broth. Cover and simmer for 15 minutes. Combine butter and flour and add to broth mixture. Stir over medium heat until mixture bubbles and thickens. Add sour cream, peas, salt, and pepper. Simmer for 5 minutes.

YIELD: 6 SERVINGS

Brussels Sprouts with Cheese Crumble

1½ pounds brussels sprouts

⅓ cup butter

1 cup cheddar cheese crackers, crushed

¼ cup Parmesan cheese, grated

Trim sprouts and cut in half. In large saucepan, cover sprouts with water, cover pan, and simmer for 15 minutes or until tender. Drain and place in warmer. Melt butter in skillet over low heat. Add crackers and stir until golden brown. Remove from heat and stir in cheese. Sprinkle over sprouts before serving.

Yield: 6 servings

Glazed Southern Sweet Potatoes

2 (16 ounce) cans sweet potatoes, drained

¾ cup pineapple or peach preserves

½ cup walnuts, chopped

1 cup mini marshmallows

1 tablespoon butter, melted

Preheat oven to 350 degrees. Arrange sweet potatoes in shallow baking dish. Spoon preserves evenly over sweet potatoes. Top with nuts, marshmallows, and butter. Bake for 25 minutes.

Yield: 6 servings

Spicy Fruit Rice

2 cups seasoned chicken broth

1½ cups instant rice

½ cup coconut, flaked

2 tablespoons butter

¼ teaspoon nutmeg

¼ teaspoon ginger

¼ teaspoon coriander

¼ teaspoon cinnamon

¼ teaspoon cloves

½ cup peaches, sliced

½ cup apricots, sliced

½ cup bananas, sliced

In small pot, bring broth to a boil. Stir in rice and coconut, cover tightly, and set aside. Melt margarine in large skillet. Add spices and stir on low heat for just a few seconds. Add fruit and simmer for 3 minutes, stirring and tossing alternately. Add rice mixture and toss.

Yield: 4 servings

Sour Cream Mushrooms

4 tablespoons butter

2 medium onions, sliced

1 pound fresh Portobello
   mushrooms

1 cup sour cream

1 teaspoon lemon juice

1 teaspoon salt

1 teaspoon pepper

In large skillet, melt butter over medium heat. Add onions and cook until limp. Stir in mushrooms and cover pan. Cook for 7 minutes over medium heat. Add sour cream, lemon juice, salt, and pepper. Simmer, stirring until sour cream is smooth and well blended.

Yield: 6 servings

Cornbread Sausage Stuffing

1 pound sausage

½ cup butter

4 cups fresh mushrooms, sliced

1 cup celery, chopped

¾ cup onion, chopped

1⅔ cups chicken broth

1 (14 ounce) package seasoned cornbread stuffing mix

1½ teaspoons poultry seasoning

In large skillet, brown sausage. Drain and pour into bowl. Set aside. Cook mushrooms, celery, and onions in butter in same skillet until tender. Add broth and simmer for 2 minutes. Stir in stuffing mix and seasoning. Stir in sausage. Pour into buttered 13 x 9-inch baking dish. Cover with foil and bake for 30 minutes. Uncover and bake for 10 minutes longer.

YIELD: 3 QUARTS

Chestnuts and Brussels Sprouts

1 pound chestnuts

2 tablespoons butter

2 tablespoons cooking sherry

1 beef bouillon cube, dissolved

1 teaspoon tomato paste

2 tablespoons cornstarch

1 cup beef broth

1 bay leaf

1 pound brussels sprouts

1 teaspoon lemon juice

Boil chestnuts in water for 2 to 3 minutes, then shell and skin them. In skillet, brown chestnuts in butter. Add sherry, stir, and remove chestnuts from pan. Add bouillon, tomato paste, and cornstarch to pan juices. Add broth slowly, stirring constantly until mixture boils. Return chestnuts to pan, along with bay leaf. Simmer until chestnuts are soft. Boil sprouts in salted water with lemon juice. Drain and add to chestnuts.

YIELD: 6 SERVINGS

Caramel Potatoes

24 small red potatoes

½ cup sugar

½ cup butter, melted

Place unpeeled potatoes in boiling water and cook for 20 minutes. Peel once cool enough to be handled. Melt sugar in heavy skillet over low heat. Cook slowly for 3 to 5 minutes, until light caramel color. Stir in melted butter. Add potatoes to pan in portions so as not to crowd them. Roll to coat on all sides. Repeat until all potatoes have been coated. Transer to serving bowl.

YIELD: 12 SERVINGS

Corn Vegetable Medley

1 (10.75 ounce) can corn soup

½ cup milk

2 cups broccoli florets

1 cup carrots, sliced

1 cup cauliflower florets

½ cup cheddar cheese, shredded

In saucepan, heat soup and milk to boiling, stirring often. Stir in vegetables. Return to boiling and cover. Cook over low heat for 20 minutes or until vegetables are tender. Stir in cheese until melted. Remove from heat.

YIELD: 6 SERVINGS

Sally's Green Bean Casserole

1 (10.75 ounce) can cream of mushroom soup

½ cup milk

1 teaspoon soy sauce

⅛ teaspoon pepper

4 cups green beans, cooked

1½ cups french-fried onions

Preheat oven to 350 degrees. In large bowl, combine soup, milk, soy sauce, pepper, green beans, and half of onions. Pour into buttered 11 x 7-inch casserole dish. Bake for 25 minutes. Sprinkle with remaining onions. Bake for 5 minutes longer.

YIELD: 6 SERVINGS

On the twelfth day of Christmas my true love sent to me. . .

Twelve Soups a-Simmering

Christmas means fellowship, feast,
giving and receiving, a time of good cheer.

Norman Vincent Peale

Dear Father, You showed us Your great love and compassion when You sent Your Son, Jesus, to rescue us from the mess we had made of our lives. During this Christmas season, and all year long, teach us to recognize those to whom we can pass along that love and compassion. There is no greater gift than the Savior. Amen.

This is how God showed his love for us: God sent his only Son into the world so we might live through him.

1 John 4:9 msg

Holiday Oyster Stew

24 ounces oysters

2 slices bacon, chopped

1 medium onion, chopped

1 (10 ounce) can cream of potato soup

1 pint half-and-half

1½ teaspoons salt

⅛ teaspoon white pepper

1 tablespoon parsley, chopped

Drain oysters, reserving liquid. Fry bacon until crisp in large skillet. Remove and drain on paper towels. Crumble bacon and set aside. Cook onion in bacon drippings until tender. Add soup, oyster liquid, half-and-half, and seasonings. Heat, stirring occasionally. Add bacon and oysters. Heat for 3 to 5 minutes longer or until oysters begin to curl. Sprinkle with parsley.

YIELD: 6 SERVINGS

Frosty Cantaloupe Soup

1 large ripe cantaloupe

½ cup dry cooking sherry

¼ cup sugar

¼ cup orange juice

Cut cantaloupe, remove seeds, and scoop out meat. Cut into chunks and place in food processor. Puree with sherry, sugar, and orange juice. Refrigerate. Best served very cold.

YIELD: 5 SERVINGS

Corn and Potato Chowder

½ cup water

3 cups frozen whole-kernel corn, thawed

1 tablespoon butter

¼ cup onion, chopped

1 garlic clove, minced

2 tablespoons flour

½ teaspoon dry mustard

¼ teaspoon salt

¼ teaspoon pepper

1 (12 ounce) can evaporated milk

1½ cups frozen hash brown potatoes

2 tablespoons fresh parsley, chopped

In food processor, combine water and 2 cups corn. Blend until smooth. Set aside. In large saucepan, melt butter over medium heat. Add onion and garlic. Cook until tender. Stir in flour, mustard, salt, and pepper. Gradually add milk. Cook, stirring constantly, until thick and bubbly. Add corn puree, remaining 1 cup corn, and hash browns. Stir well and cook over low heat for 15 minutes. Garnish with fresh parsley.

YIELD: 4 SERVINGS

Turkey Giblet Soup

1 turkey carcass

Giblets, neck, and liver from 1 turkey

2 onions, diced

4 whole cloves

1 bay leaf

½ teaspoon black pepper, coarsely ground

2 quarts water

1 quart chicken broth

1 leek, diced

1 carrot, diced

1 celery stalk, diced

1 teaspoon fresh thyme, chopped

1 teaspoon fresh parsley, chopped

½ cup shell pasta

1 teaspoon salt

1 teaspoon pepper

In large kettle, combine turkey carcass, giblets, neck, liver, onions, cloves, bay leaf, pepper, water, and chicken broth. Cover and simmer for 2 hours. Strain broth into large saucepan. Chop giblets, neck meat, and liver. Add to broth. Add leek, carrot, celery, thyme, parsley, and pasta. Stir and simmer uncovered for 25 minutes. Stir in salt and pepper.

YIELD: 8 SERVINGS

Salmon and Corn Chowder

3 tablespoons butter

1 small onion, chopped

4 cups half-and-half

1 (15.75 ounce) can whole-kernel corn, drained

1 (14.75 ounce) can cream-style corn

¾ teaspoon salt

¼ teaspoon garlic powder

⅛ teaspoon pepper

1 pound fresh or frozen salmon fillets, thawed

Heat 2 tablespoons butter in large pot over medium heat. Add onion and cook, stirring often, for 5 minutes or until onion is softened. Add half-and-half, whole corn, cream corn, salt, garlic powder, pepper, and remaining 1 tablespoon butter. Cook until mixture begins to simmer. Do not boil. Add salmon and cook for 2 minutes.

YIELD: 4 SERVINGS

Pumpkin Soup

2 quarts pumpkin, peeled and seeded

2 quarts chicken broth

2 cups heavy cream

½ teaspoon salt

½ teaspoon nutmeg

½ teaspoon pepper

In large kettle, combine pumpkin and chicken broth. Cover and simmer until tender (40 to 50 minutes). Cool and puree in blender. Return to kettle, add remaining ingredients, and mix well.

YIELD: 8 SERVINGS

Tasty Turkey Soup

2 tablespoons butter

1 pound cubed turkey

⅔ cup uncooked quick-cooking barley

2 (14.5 ounce) cans beef broth

2 (16 ounce) cans whole tomatoes, undrained

2 cups fresh mixed vegetables

Melt butter in Dutch oven. Brown turkey cubes in butter. Stir in barley, broth, and tomatoes. Heat to boiling, stirring occasionally. Add vegetables. Boil for 15 minutes. Reduce heat and simmer for 25 minutes or until barley and vegetables are tender.

Yield: 6 servings

Crab Bisque

- - - ❄ - - - ❄ - - - ❄ - - - ❄ - - -

8 ounces jumbo lump crabmeat

1 teaspoon salt

⅛ teaspoon pepper

¼ teaspoon thyme

Bay leaf

1 cup rice

½ cup heavy cream

2 tablespoons small croutons

Remove any bones or ligaments from crabmeat. Place crabmeat, seasonings, and rice in 2 quarts boiling water and cook for 5 minutes. Lower temperature to simmer and cover, cooking for 1 hour. Remove from heat and cool. Shortly before serving, add cream and sprinkle with croutons.

YIELD: 6 SERVINGS

Pea Soup

2 cups dried peas

2 quarts water

1 small onion, sliced

2 tablespoons butter

½ teaspoon salt

¼ teaspoon pepper

6 tablespoons croutons

Wash peas, drain, and cover with cold water. Allow to soak overnight. Drain and place in 3-quart kettle. Add water, onion, butter, salt, and pepper. Cover and boil slowly for 3 to 4 hours. Puree in food processor. Return to kettle and reheat. Garnish with croutons.

YIELD: 6 SERVINGS

Potato Soup with Sour Cream

2 cups potatoes, diced

1 cup boiling water

1 teaspoon salt

1 small onion, sliced

½ teaspoon pepper

2 cups sour cream

1 tablespoon parsley, minced

In large saucepan or kettle, combine potatoes, water, salt, onion, and pepper. Cook for 20 minutes. Add cream and cook until potatoes are tender. Garnish with parsley.

YIELD: 4 SERVINGS

Cream of Artichoke Soup

2 tablespoons onion, finely chopped

¼ cup butter

2 tablespoons flour

½ cup milk

1 (14 ounce) can artichoke hearts,
cut up, juice reserved

1 (14 ounce) can chicken broth

3 egg yolks

½ cup heavy cream

1 teaspoon lemon juice

¼ teaspoon nutmeg

¼ teaspoon salt

2 tablespoons, chopped parsley

Sauté onion in butter until transparent. Add flour, stirring until light brown. With mixer, blend milk, juice from artichokes, and chicken broth into flour mixture. Bring to a boil. In bowl, mix egg yolks and cream. Beat yolk mixture into soup with mixer to combine. Lower heat. Add lemon juice and nutmeg. Continue beating with mixer until well blended. Add artichokes and salt. Garnish with parsley.

YIELD: 6 SERVINGS

French Onion Soup

2 large onions, thinly sliced

2 tablespoons butter

2 cups beef broth

½ cup heavy cream

½ teaspoon salt

¼ teaspoon pepper

1 teaspoon Worcestershire sauce

4 thin bread slices

½ cup Parmesan cheese

Sauté onion in butter until light brown. Add broth and bring to a boil. Boil for 10 minutes. Add cream, salt, and pepper. Before serving, stir in Worcestershire sauce. Sprinkle bread with cheese and place under oven broiler until lightly browned. Place slice of toast in each bowl before pouring soup in.

YIELD: 4 SERVINGS

Our Family Favorite Recipes

Recipe Index

Appetizers

Beverages

Breads

Breakfast Dishes

Candies

Cookies

Desserts

Kids' Recipes

Main Dishes

Salads

Sides

Soups